HOW TO GUIDE
GIRL SCOUT BROWNIES THROUGH

WOW!
WONDERS OF WATER

IT'S YOUR PLANET—LOVE IT! A LEADERSHIP JOURNEY

A Girl Scout leadership journey invites girls to explore a theme
through many experiences and from many perspectives.
All the joys of travel are built right in: meeting new people, exploring new things,
making memories, gathering keepsakes. This guide is your suitcase.
It's packed with everything you need for a wonderful trip that will change girls' lives.

Girl Scouts of the USA

CHAIR,
NATIONAL BOARD
OF DIRECTORS
Connie L. Lindsey

CHIEF
EXECUTIVE
OFFICER
Kathy Cloninger

VICE
PRESIDENT,
PROGRAM
Eileen Doyle

Girl Scouts.

WRITING TEAM: Laura Tuchman, Anne Marie Welsh, Leigh Fenley

CONTRIBUTORS: Toi James, Kate Gottlieb, Kathleen Sweeney

ILLUSTRATED BY Helena Garcia

DESIGNED BY Alexander Isley Inc.

MANAGER, OPERATIONS: Sharon Kaplan

GSUSA DESIGN TEAM: Sarah Micklem, Rocco Alberico

© 2009 by Girl Scouts of the USA

First published in 2009 by Girl Scouts of the USA
420 Fifth Avenue, New York, NY 10018-2798
www.girlscouts.org

ISBN: 978-0-88441-738-5

Printed in Italy

1 2 3 4 5 6 7 8 9/17 16 15 14 13 12 11 10 09

Page 38: Photo courtesy of Water for People.

Page 65: Activities adapted from resources created for an African Water Awareness Event sponsored by Girl Scouts, San Diego/Imperial Council.

Text printed on Fredrigoni Cento
40 percent de-inked, post-consumer
fibers and 60 percent secondary
recycled fibers.

Covers printed on Prisma artboard
FSC Certified mixed sources.

CONTENTS

"With every breath you take, every drop of water you drink . . . you are connected to the ocean and to life in the ocean."

—Sylvia Earle, oceanographer, speaking on the Weather Channel's "Forecast Earth," 2008

Welcome to *WOW!*

On our Blue Planet, water is a life-giving force.
It's also a maker of rainbows.

Straightforward facts and breathtaking natural wonders—that's the mix at the heart of this Girl Scout leadership journey all about water.

WOW! calls on Brownies across the country and around the world to use their leadership skills and values to protect the waters of Planet Earth. The journey invites girls to engage their minds and hearts as they explore the *Wonders of Water*. What they learn about water, and the awe that this new knowledge inspires, will be the springboard to caring about this precious resource now and throughout their lives.

The girls are joining an enduring tradition, and so are you. The wonders of the natural world and the need to care for them have been at the core of Girl Scouting since its founding in 1912. One early Brownie Scout Handbook noted, "Nature is everywhere all the time—in cities, in the woods and fields, in the winter, spring, summer, and fall."

That's the spirit of this journey, too: Water is everywhere.

Wowing Brownies with Two WOWs

To engage Brownies, this fun and fact-filled journey uses two kinds of WOWs. The first stands for Wonders of Water—the many forms and paths that water takes in the world and the awesomeness of it in our lives. The second stands for Ways of Working. These WOWs give Brownies opportunities to role-play and learn as they engage in teamwork, effective speaking, and educating and inspiring others.

Together these WOWs help girls develop into leaders who understand the importance of water and the right of everyone and everything to enjoy this precious resource. The Brownies will come to know how they can protect water and advocate for others to do so, too. And they'll be leaders who can take on the challenge of making a difference in any arena they choose.

HEARTS AND MINDS

So much information is now available about environmental problems facing our planet and what must be done to correct them. *WOW!* is part of a series of Girl Scout leadership journeys that invites girls, and their families and adult volunteers, to make sense of that information so they can act for the betterment of Earth.

The umbrella theme for the series, It's Your Planet—Love It!, came directly from a brainstorm with teen girls. Its sentiment is clear: The desire to nurture and protect is first and foremost an act of love. If girls love Planet Earth and all its wonders—watery and otherwise—they will naturally be moved to protect it. Love for Planet Earth is the true and necessary starting point for thoughtful and sustained environmental action.

You may already be deeply committed to environmental causes—or not. Either way, you will be guiding girls on a journey of learning and doing that creates larger ripples in their lives and in the world.

YOU'RE ON THIS JOURNEY, TOO!

As you guide girls to Take Action to protect the world's water, you may find yourself adjusting some of your own water habits. If you do, you'll be adding to the ripples the girls create. And you'll see that as the girls work to create ripples in the world, every water droplet counts. In the end, those ripples might just become powerful waves!

All along its watery route, *WOW!* engages girls in science, math, the outdoors, and environmental stewardship. You may be an expert in one or all of these areas—or none. No matter—there's no need to have all the answers! All you need to guide your group of Brownies is right here in this book. Just add your own sense of wonder, and an eagerness to explore all that water offers and accomplishes in partnership with Brownies.

Imagine the power of 800,000 Brownies and their volunteers and families making choices that conserve and protect Earth's water. What are you waiting for? Dive right in!

Snapshot of the Journey

SESSION 1

Loving Water

The Brownies begin exploring the Wonders of Water, what they LOVE about water, and why it's important to protect water. They:

- Start a Team WOW Map showing what they love about water
- Think about how people use water around the world
- Begin to get ideas about what they can do as individuals to protect water
- Investigate the science and wonder of rainbows

SESSION 2

"Green" Tea for a Blue Planet

Through a festive tea party, the Brownies learn about the water cycle. They realize that everyone on Earth shares water, and that's why it's so important to save and protect it. The girls:

- Talk about their favorite water places—and add them to their Team WOW Map
- Explore the water cycle
- Go home to make and carry out a promise to protect water

SESSION 3

Water for All

The Brownies report back on how they carried out their promises to protect water and earn their LOVE Water awards. They then engage in water-gathering and rationing activities to experience how families make do in places where clean water is scarce. This deepens the Brownies' understanding of the importance of saving Earth's water. The girls:

- Collect their "water drops," which represent what they have done individually to protect water, and add them to their Team WOW Map
- Experience what it's like to gather and ration water

SESSION 4

Teaming Up to Advocate for Water

The Brownies create a team plan to SAVE water. They:

- Think about all the ways people use water
- Develop a plan for one way to ask people to SAVE water
- Make a team decision about choosing and carrying out their plan

SESSION 5
Advocates Communicate!

The Brownies prepare to carry out their SAVE project as a team. They might also be learning more about their water issue through a guest visitor or even a field trip. The girls:

- Practice WOWing others with great communication skills
- Share their hopes for what their SAVE project will accomplish

SESSION 6
SAVE!

The Brownie Team advocates for saving water! The girls:

- Carry out their SAVE project

SESSION 7
Planning to SHARE

The Brownies discuss the success of their SAVE effort and what they learned from it. They earn their SAVE Water awards and get creative as they plan to educate and inspire more people to protect water. The girls:

- Brainstorm about who can join them in their effort to SAVE water
- Develop a creative way to inspire others to join in their effort
- Consider how their efforts are like drops flowing to a river—and getting ready to meet the ocean!

SESSION 8
SHARE!

The Brownies SHARE what they've learned and how they have acted to SAVE water with others (younger kids, family members, school, community). They invite their guests to take action for water. The girls:

- Lead their guests in an opening ceremony to experience the power of a river meeting the ocean
- Use and show what they know to inspire others to commit to SAVE water
- Have their guests make a commitment to act for water
- Earn the SHARE Water award

SESSION 9
WOW!

The Brownies reflect on their journey—from loving water as individuals, to saving water as a team, to sharing what they know with even more people and inviting them to protect water, too. The girls receive their WOW! awards. During this closing gathering, the girls:

- Celebrate with watery treats and water friends
- Imagine what they will do on future Girl Scout adventures

Awards Along the Journey

Brownies have the opportunity to earn four prestigious leadership awards as they seek new challenges on this *WOW!* journey. The steps to the awards, which are woven directly into the Sample Sessions, begin with small, personal acts and then move out to purposeful teamwork that engages the larger community and influences its members in significant ways. You might think of the Brownie award steps as flowing like water: What begins as a small stream flows into a river, and that mighty river then flows into the sea, creating waves of lasting influence. Here are the four awards and the steps to earning them:

LOVE Water: This first award encourages girls to become aware of the many ways they use and enjoy water. As they begin to understand the science of water and its importance in the world, they will also make a personal commitment to protect it. To earn the award, the girls:

- Show two things they know and love about water.
- Make and carry out one personal promise that protects water.

The steps to this award are built into the suggested activities in Sample Sessions 1, 2, and 3. In Session 2, the girls will share their water promises, and in Session 3 they will talk about how they carried through on those promises.

SAVE Water: The second award is earned when the Brownies team up and speak up as advocates to protect water or keep it clean in their community. Many project ideas are on pages 56–59 of the girls' book and also in Sample Session 4, where the girls start thinking as a team about what they will do for water. By making an effort that moves beyond themselves, the girls begin to realize the impact that group efforts can produce.

SHARE Water: Girls earn the third award as they create an even bigger ripple by sharing their efforts for water with others, educating and inspiring them to join in, and asking them to commit to a water promise. (Suggestions for how to educate and inspire others are on pages 56–59 and 100–101 of the girls' book, and on page 74 and 84 of this guide.)

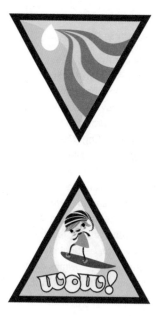

WOW! Girls culminate their journey by earning the WOW! Award, a grand finale that symbolizes the powerful change they've brought to their community. They earn the award by showing proof of their SHARE Water efforts, and by describing how their efforts relate to the Girl Scout Law and how they have had an impact as leaders. (Suggested ways for the girls to obtain "proof" of their influence are on page 75 of this guide.)

IF A GIRL MISSES AN AWARD STEP . . .

Find a way for her to do something similar to what she missed so she can still earn the award with her Brownie group. Your goal is to guide her to have the same learning and growing opportunity—and to understand how she can contribute to the team. You might call on the full Brownie team to brainstorm about how girls who miss steps can best get back on track with the journey.

If a girl misses the day that the Brownies head home to take part in a family activity, she can do the activity after a later session and still share her results with the team. If a girl forgets to bring back an activity, or her family hasn't had a chance to do it with her, she can do it at a later time. Or help her think of other ways to accomplish something similar.

Girls may not experience activities in exactly the same way, but they can each take away new insights, connections, and a sense of accomplishment.

PROJECT IDEAS? DON'T WORRY!

Plenty of ideas are built into the girls' book and the journey's sample sessions. Plus, the girls are bound to have many more!

Their efforts for water may get a whole ocean of people working together for water!

Health, Safety, and Well-Being

SAFETY FIRST

Seek out the Girl Scout Safety Activity Checkpoints from your council and keep them handy. They detail the safety net provided for girls in Girl Scouting. Use them along with any additional information from your council to plan trips and activities, and to promote the well-being of the girls every time you get together. They will be particularly useful as the Brownies carry out their SAVE and SHARE projects.

The emotional and physical safety and well-being of girls is of paramount importance in Girl Scouting. Look out for the safety of girls by following the Girl Scout Activity Checkpoints when planning all gatherings and trips, and:

- Check into any additional safety guidelines your council might provide
- Talk to girls and their families about special needs or concerns

Welcoming Girls with Disabilities

Girl Scouting embraces girls with many different needs and is guided by a very specific and positive philosophy of inclusion that benefits all: Each girl is an equal and valued member of a group with typically developing peers.

As an adult volunteer, you have the chance to improve the way society views girls with disabilities. One way to start is with language. Your words have a huge impact on the process of inclusion. People-First Language puts the person before the disability:

FIRE SAFETY

Young girls can be taught to start a camp fire under the watchful supervision of an adult. Be mindful of local bans on building fires and policies on open flames. It's always possible to enjoy a simulated, no-flame campfire!

SAY	INSTEAD OF
She has autism.	She's autistic.
She has an intellectual disability.	She's mentally retarded.
She has a learning disability.	The girl is learning-disabled.
She uses a wheelchair.	She is wheelchair-bound.
She has a disability.	She is handicapped.

LEARN WHAT A GIRL NEEDS

First, don't assume that because a person has a disability, she needs assistance or special accommodations. Probably the most important thing you can do is to ask the individual girl or her parents or guardians what she needs to make her experience in Girl Scouts successful. If you are frank with the girl and her parents and make yourself accessible to them, it's likely they will respond in kind, creating a better experience for all.

It's important for all girls to be rewarded based on their best efforts—not on completion of a task. Give any girl the opportunity to do her best and she will. Sometimes that means changing a few rules or approaching an activity in a more creative way. Here are a few examples:

- Invite a girl to perform an activity after observing others doing it first.

- Ask the girls to come up with ideas on how to adapt an activity.

- Often what counts most is staying flexible and varying your approach. For a list of resources, visit www.girlscouts.org and search on "disability resources."

GIRL SCOUT COUNCIL CONTACT INFO

Name: _____

_____

_____

Can help with: _____

_____

_____

Phone: _____

E-mail: _____

Snacking Smart Along *WOW!*

If the Brownies meet after school, they'll likely need a snack. Encourage members of your Brownie Friends and Family Network to take turns providing snacks. Watery treats will be fun for the journey—and are generally healthful, too. Ideas for festive watery snacks are offered throughout the sessions and in the girls' book. Consider asking Network members to bring:

- Slices of fruit floating in a pitcher of water

- Slices of different melons or fruits

Check in with Brownie families about any food allergies or food issues.

A New Brownie Story to Share and Cherish

READ THE STORY AS YOU DIVE INTO WOW!

You'll find it helpful to take time to read the full story on your own before your real-life Brownie journey begins. (Try it with a "watery" snack—herbal tea, perhaps?) Reading ahead will give you time to reflect on the best use of the story with your group of girls.

Brownie stories featuring a magical elf are a beloved Girl Scout tradition that reaches back to the earliest Brownies. In this *WOW!* journey, a new Brownie story, "A Very Wet ELF Adventure," stars Brownie Elf and friends Alejandra, Campbell, and Jamila. The Brownies in your group may have met them on the *Brownie Quest* or they'll meet them here for the first time. Either way, encourage the girls to jump right in and explore along with Brownie Elf and the three friends.

In the story, Brownie Elf and the girls enjoy a series of water adventures that introduce them to four wonders of water: the water cycle, wetlands, the deep sea, and waterpower. Throughout these adventures, the elf continues to play her historic role: inspiring girls to see that they are capable of extraordinary things, especially if they work together.

INSPIRATION FOR REAL-LIFE ACTION

The give-and-take in the friendship of the fictional girls, their curiosity and willingness to learn, their caring, and their commitment to do something to save water and keep it pure are meant to be a springboard to exploration and action for real-life Brownies. Although real-life Brownies can't do exactly what the fictional characters do, many of the activities and explorations suggested in the Sample Sessions in this guide are designed to engage girls in wonders similar to those in the ELF Adventure.

MAKING THE MOST OF THE ELF ADVENTURE

- You and the real Brownies might decide to read the ELF Adventure together as a group.

- Or maybe the girls want to act out scenes with help from volunteers or older Girl Scouts (maybe even a Cadette earning her LiA Award). Or perhaps the Brownies want to act out a scene for their Daisy sisters!

- If girls are interested, include a story time at the start of each session.

- Or add a session or two devoted exclusively to the story. Discussion questions tied to the story and its related water topics are sprinkled throughout the Sample Sessions.

- No matter how your group decides to enjoy the ELF Adventure, girls will be able to relate their own water experiences to its colorful scenes as they seek out special water places and water issues in their own lives. For example, Brownie Elf and the fictional Brownie friends watch a rainstorm, visit a wetland, explore deep-sea creatures, and see a dam up close. These are all possibilities for real Brownie excursions, too.

- Encourage families to enjoy the story with their Brownies, and to talk together about how the adventures tie in to what the girls are doing in their Brownie group.

S.S. BROWNIE

The WOWs of Math and Science

Walks along the beach, stream explorations, puddle stomping—all of these Brownie-friendly activities engage girls in understanding the scientific fact that Planet Earth is mostly made of water. Water of all kinds—marshes, ponds, lakes, and pools—sparks the curiosity of young girls. It may even be that water holds a universal fascination for all of us—girls included—because we are made up mostly of H_2O!

As the Brownies learn about water all around them, you and they will see that science and math are part of daily life. Yet a troublesome gap often develops between girls' interest and ability in science and math and their desire and confidence to pursue higher education, and ultimately careers, in these fields. To sustain interest and build confidence, Girl Scouts believes that early exposure to the joys and wonders of these subjects is crucial—as is encouragement from families, teachers, and the media that is so much a part of daily life.

BUILDING SCIENTIFIC MINDS

On this journey, girls experience how essential the sciences and math are to any desire to protect Planet Earth. This journey fosters lifelong interests in those subjects—and every wonder of water: wetlands and waves, deep-sea exploration, even the small, daily dramas of weather. In fact, experiencing weather in all its forms is a perfect way to introduce the science of water to second- and third-graders. Mist on the pond? Water vapor. Rivers and streams running fast after a rain? Water in motion. Skating on a frozen pond? Water as solid ice.

Take advantage of each time that science and math pop up in the girls' lives. Checking an outdoor weather thermometer each morning? The start of meteorology. Spying a stranded jellyfish on the beach? Marine biology. Opening your eyes underwater? Oceanography. Clean drinking water from the tap? Engineering! Even the blurred effect of watercolor paint on paper opens the way to discussions about the science of water.

TAKE TIME TO MEET INSPIRING WOMEN

The women profiled throughout *WOW!* offer opportunities for girls to meet and be inspired by scientists, engineers, and others working in environmental fields.

Use these profiles as stepping-stones to engage your group of Brownies in their own real-life meetings with inspiring women in their community.

TUNE IN TO EVERYDAY SCIENCE

Many kitchen activities involve water transformations, too. Using a lid to cover a pot and quicken water boiling time is a way to speed the process of liquid water becoming vapor. Baking a cake combines chemistry and a lot of math—ratios, measurements, proportions. What's a measuring cup, after all, but a basic math tool? A flattened cake pulled from the oven might signal a scientific misfire. Not enough eggs, perhaps? Or no baking powder? Experienced chefs might dispense with measuring tools, but even the most intuitive cooks remain attuned to science.

So make the most of every creative scientific moment that arises. If you and the girls leave jars outside to measure rainfall, be on the lookout for rainbows when you collect them. You'll see one if the returning sunshine strikes water droplets at just the right angle. On this journey, you and the girls can take in the full details of a rainbow's creation—or you can simply enjoy the wonder of it all and say WOW!

Brownies and the Great Outdoors

Brownie-age girls have enough energy to fuel nearly any outdoor adventure. They're natural treasure hunters and explorers and more than ready to sing in the rain, marvel at a frozen lake, or gaze at eerie fog rising among the trees. Enjoying the outdoors is the foundation for a lasting love and repect for nature, so consider inviting the Brownies on a range of outdoor excursions:

- **Day trips to local nature areas**, including wetlands (swamps, marshlands, bayous, and bogs all qualify), let girls experience the natural world of their region firsthand.

- **Parks, gardens, natural history museums, and zoos** are among the great urban places for enriching and possibly water-filled adventures. There's no limit to what the girls can explore in them. They might, for example, check out any water fountains they see. Are they working? Are people using them? If not, why not? How does the water come out? In dribbles or bursts? As a group, they might ask a few questions of other people they see out and about on their own outdoor adventures.

- **Neighborhood walks, including puddle-hopping** in a mild rainstorm, offer opportunities for the girls to explore the watery riches of their streets and sidewalks. Seeing water carry sticks and leaves into storm drains, and rainwater cascade into runoff, are cues to this journey's opening question, "Where does all the water go?"

SPONTANEOUS BOAT-BUILDING

When visiting ponds or other waterways, the girls might enjoy making simple boats from found materials, such as fallen leaves. Just be sure to drive home the point that live plants should not be disturbed. Invite each girl to:

- Choose two large leaves, one for the boat's body and one for the sail.

- Find a small stick for the mast.

- Thread the stick through the sail and then stick it into the bottom of the boat.

- Launch the boat and watch it catch the wind, spin on the eddies, or capsize!

Camping

For some Brownies, overnight camping will be a new experience. A first campout might be in a backyard or a local park in a family camp setting. In some regions, sleepover camp of up to two weeks is also an option for Brownies.

A camp readiness quiz can help girls and their parents determine if the experience is appropriate for them. Check with your council for details.

BEFORE VENTURING OUTDOORS . . .

Follow the Girl Scout motto: Be prepared! Talk to the Brownies about how to treat plants and animals with care:

- **Teach Leave No Trace principles**, which include never taking live vegetation or animals from their habitat.

- **Talk about what "Do Not Disturb" means** with plants and animals: *Would it include not flipping over rocks to look underneath? Not pulling up moss? Not ripping leaves from bushes? Not stomping on holes that might house animals or insects?*

CAMP MEMORIES: WORKING WAYS OF WEE ANTS

"I spotted some of the girls stamping the ground furiously, and went to investigate. They were stomping a trail of ants! I asked, "Have you discovered where they're going?" A look of confusion; it hadn't occurred to the girls that the ants were actually going somewhere. We crouched to watch and the girls became enchanted. Soon they were dropping tiny crumbs for the ants—to watch them drag the crumb back home. We talked about how they worked together on larger crumbs, and how everyone 'at home' would get to share."

—Tia Ramsey, Girl Scouts of Western North Carolina, Pisgah Council, recalling her group of Brownies camping in a national forest

Making the Most of Brownies' Skills

When planning outdoor adventures, be aware that second- and third-graders:

Like to run, walk, and play in groups.	*So they are more than ready for hiking.*
Need clear directions and like structure.	*So first make a plan for an outing in familiar territory. When trying someplace new, have the girls brainstorm the rules for group travel before they go. Add in any rules they miss.*
Can tie things and use tools.	*So introduce simple projects, like making boats from natural materials.*
Are comfortable with number concepts, time, and distance.	*So they can grasp simple mapmaking, calculating distances, and the four directions.*
Love to playact.	*So they might like to create plays with animal and tree characters. Showtime at the campfire? Some national and state parks have amphitheaters you can use.*
Are generally cooperative and know how to follow rules, and listen to adults.	*So the respect you show for the natural world will carry forward. If they learn not to snap branches from living trees, and to respect animal habitats, they will teach others as well.*

In groups with both second- and third-graders, skills may vary. So encourage older girls to mentor younger ones.

Girl Scout Traditions and Ceremonies

Celebrating Girl Scout traditions connects girls to one another, to their sister Girl Scouts and Girl Guides around the world, and to the generations of girls who were Girl Scouts before them.

Along *WOW!*, you'll notice frequent opportunities to sing, gather in Brownie Friendship Circles, and hold award ceremonies. Your Girl Scout council might celebrate other traditions that you can incorporate into *WOW!*, too. Here are a few of the most enduring Girl Scout traditions:

GIRL SCOUT SIGN

The Girl Scout sign is made when you say the Girl Scout Promise. The sign is formed with the right hand, by using the thumb to hold down the little finger, leaving the three middle fingers extended to represent the three parts of the Promise.

QUIET SIGN

The Quiet Sign is a way to silence a crowd without shouting at anyone. The sign is made by holding up the right hand with all five fingers extended. It refers to the original Fifth Law of Girl Scouting: A Girl Scout is courteous.

GIRL SCOUT HANDSHAKE

The Girl Scout handshake is the way many Girl Guides and Girl Scouts greet each other. They shake their left hands while making the Girl Scout sign with their right hand.

FRIENDSHIP CIRCLE

The Friendship Circle is often formed at the end of meetings or campfires as a closing ceremony. Everyone gathers in a circle, and each girl crosses her right arm over her left and holds hands with the person on each side. Once everyone is silent, the leader starts the friendship squeeze by squeezing the hand of the person next to her. One by one, each girl passes on the squeeze until it travels around the full circle.

What + How: Creating a Quality Experience

I t's not just *what* girls do, but *how* you engage them that creates a high-quality experience. All Girl Scout activities are built on three processes—Girl Led, Learning by Doing, and Cooperative Learning—that make Girl Scouting unique from school and other extracurricular activities. When used together, these processes ensure the quality and promote the fun and friendship so integral to Girl Scouting. Take some time to understand these processes and how to use them with Brownies.

Girl Led

"Girl Led" is just what it sounds like—girls play an active part in figuring out the what, where, when, how, and why of their activities. So encourage them to lead the planning, decision-making, learning, and fun as much as possible. This ensures that girls are engaged in their learning and experience leadership opportunities as they prepare to become active participants in their local and global communities. With Brownies, you could:

- Help girls make informed choices by talking them through the various steps of decision-making

- Encourage girls to be creative and add their own flair to projects and activities

- Look for opportunities to role-play problem-solving and give girls the freedom to solve problems on their own

Learning by Doing

Learning by Doing is a hands-on learning process that engages girls in continuous cycles of action and reflection that result in deeper understanding of concepts and mastery of practical skills. As they participate in meaningful activities and then reflect on them, girls get to explore their own questions, discover answers, gain new skills, and share ideas and observations with others. Throughout the process, it's important for girls to be able to connect their experiences to their lives and apply what they have learned to their future experiences both within and outside of Girl Scouting. With Brownies, you could:

KEEP IT GIRL LED

From beginning to end, keep your eye on what the girls want to do and the direction they seem to be taking. It's the approach begun by Juliette Gordon Low: When she and her associates couldn't decide on a new direction, she often said, "Let's ask the girls!"

Girl Led experiences are built right into *WOW!* to make it easy for you. For example, during Session 5, the girls role-play good and not-so-good ways to communicate and then come up with their own "Top Tips" for advocating. They also take the lead in sorting through the best project ideas for their SAVE and SHARE awards.

At each session, ask the girls for any last thoughts on what they've done or discussed.

- Encourage girls to answer some of their own questions through hands-on activities

- Ask girls to do more than they are capable of doing on their own while giving them limited but strategic help

- Offer opportunities for girls to explore the natural world that engage their motor skills and their senses (see page 18 for suggestions).

For the Brownie Team, this means giving the girls (and yourself!) some quiet time throughout the journey to stop, think, talk, and reflect. Resist the urge to rush from "doing" to "more doing," and try to follow the discussion tips and questions provided to assist the Brownies in getting deeper meaning from what they have just done.

Cooperative Learning

Through cooperative learning, girls work together toward shared goals in an atmosphere of respect and collaboration that encourages the sharing of skills, knowledge, and learning. Moreover, given that many girls desire to connect with others, cooperative learning may be a particularly meaningful and enjoyable way to engage girls in learning. Working together in all-girl environments also encourages girls to feel powerful and emotionally and physically safe, and it allows them to experience a sense of belonging, even in the most diverse groups. With Brownies, you could:

- Make the most of teamwork activities, and create other enjoyable activities throughout Girl Scouting that girls have to accomplish in teams

- Encourage girls to take responsibility as a team for deciding how to accomplish a task

- Demonstrate giving others equal opportunity to participate in group decisions

LEARNING BY DOING ON THEIR OWN

The girls have even more opportunities to reflect on their journey experiences and apply them to their lives through activities in their book. For example, on page 77, they think about how, in the ELF Adventure, Brownie Elf keeps her promise to take the Brownie friends on a water adventure. Then the girls are asked to reflect on when and how they keep promises in their own lives, why that is important, and how keeping promises relates to the values of the Girl Scout Law.

WOWS FOR TEAMWORK

Throughout the journey the girls take part in Ways of Working (WOW) activities that build teamwork and cooperation. Starting in Session 1, the Brownies also begin a team effort to map all their Wonders of Water. Throughout the journey, you might ask each girl to reflect on how her teammates' additions to the map have expanded her view of water in the world.

Seeing Girl Scout Processes Play Out in a *WOW!* Activity

Girl Scout processes play out in a variety of ways during team gatherings, but often they are so seamless you might not notice them. For example, in Session 5 (page 79), the Brownies plan their SAVE project. The call-outs below show how the Girl Scout processes make this activity a learning and growing experience for girls—and up the fun, too! Throughout *WOW!*, you'll see processes and outcomes play out again and again. Before you know it, you'll be using these valuable aspects of Girl Scouting in whatever Brownies do—from earning a Try-It to planning a trip.

Preparing to SAVE

Now the girls will likely need time to create materials or presentations for their team SAVE effort. They might be designing signs to hang in a school about not running water longer than needed, practicing how to ask people to use refillable water bottles, or making a presentation to ask everyone in their neighborhood to check for leaks.

> This is an example of the **Girl Led** process. The girls are taking the lead on deciding what their presentations will be and what their signs will look like for the SAVE effort. That they are making their own signs is also an example of **Learning by Doing.**

> Practicing is an example of **Learning by Doing.** This activity is also an example of the Take Action outcome **Girls educate and inspire others to act**—when the girls practice various ways to get their message across to people in their neighborhood to SAVE water by checking for leaks.

- Assist the girls as they get organized to work on whatever might be needed for the team's SAVE efforts—signs, booklets, a skit, etc.

- Or invite the girls to talk with a special visitor whose work or volunteer effort is related to the Brownie Team's SAVE project. For example, perhaps someone from the local water utility.

As the Brownies plan their effort, guide them to promote good teamwork by:

- Encouraging them to take turns
- Making sure each girl has a role
- Praising girls when you observe great cooperation

BE KIND TO WATER!

When volunteers assist girls with their SAVE projects by helping them organize their efforts, that's **Girl Led** at the Brownie grade level. Girls at this age are able to take the lead on decision-making, but they might need help carrying out their plans.

When girls seek out community members to get more information on a topic of their choice, or to partner with them on a Take Action project such as their SAVE effort, they are moving toward the Connect outcome of **Girls feel connected to their communities, locally and globally.**

This section is an excellent example of the Connect outcome **Girls promote cooperation and team-building.** As Brownies work together on their SAVE projects, they start to fine-tune their cooperation and team-building skills. All of this is achieved through the **Cooperative Learning** process, as girls work together on the common goal of their SAVE project.

Understanding the Journey's Leadership Benefits

Filled with fun and friendship, *WOW!* is designed to develop the skills and values young girls need to be leaders now and as they grow. *WOW!* activities are designed to enable Brownies to achieve 10 of 15 national outcomes, or benefits, of the Girl Scout Leadership Experience, as summarized on the next page.

Each girl is different, so don't expect them all to exhibit the same signs to indicate what they are learning along the journey. What matters is that you are guiding the Brownies toward leadership skills and qualities they can use right now—and all their lives.

For full definitions of the outcomes and the signs that Girl Scout Brownies are achieving them, see *Transforming Leadership: Focusing on Outcomes of the New Girl Scout Leadership Experience* (GSUSA, 2008). Keep in mind that the intended benefits to girls are the cumulative result of traveling through an entire journey—and everything else girls experience in Girl Scouting.

FOCUS OF GIRL SCOUT ACTIVITIES

Discover
Connect
Take Action

GIRL SCOUT PROCESSES

Girl Led
Learning by Doing
Cooperative Learning

15 SHORT-TERM AND INTERMEDIATE OUTCOMES

Girls gain specific knowledge, skills, attitudes, behaviors, and values in Girl Scouting.

LONG-TERM OUTCOME

Girls lead with courage, confidence, and character, to make the world a better place.

NATIONAL LEADERSHIP OUTCOMES

		AT THE BROWNIE LEVEL, girls...	RELATED ACTIVITIES (by Session number or girls' book part/page)	SAMPLE "SIGN" When the outcome is achieved, girls might...
DISCOVER	**Girls develop a strong sense of self.**	have increased confidence in their abilities	S5: Communicate It!; GB, P2 and P4: WOW	express pride in their accomplishments when speaking with others.
	Girls develop positive values.	begin to apply values inherent in the Girl Scout Promise and Law in various contexts.	S1: Protecting Water and Living the GS Law; 2: Loving and Protecting Water: Continuing the Conversation; S3, 8, and 9: Opening Ceremonies. GB P3: WOW, p. 77; P4: Mottos & Secret Words	explain how they will take responsibility on the playground, at home, and at school.
		are better able to examine positive and negative effects of people's actions on others and the environment.	S1: Thinking About Water, Protecting Water; Living the GS Law; S2: "Green" Tea; S3: Our Team WOW Map. GB: WOW Wisdom quizzes; P2: How I Use Water	provide alternative choices to actions that harm the environment.
	Girls seek challenges in the world.	are more open to learning or doing new and challenging things.	Planning and carrying out the SAVE and SHARE projects; S4: Opening Ceremony	enjoy trying new activities.
		recognize that one can learn from mistakes.		feel it is OK to make mistakes and might describe an instance in their own lives where they learned from a mistake.
CONNECT	**Girls develop healthy relationships.**	begin to understand how their behavior contributes to maintaining healthy relationships.	GB, p. 21: WOW	can identify healthy/unhealthy behaviors (honesty, caring, bullying, etc.) when presented with a relationship scenario.
		are better able to show empathy toward others.	GB, p. 33: WOW: Exploring People's Differences	make empathetic statements and/or report being more caring in their interactions with others.
	Girls promote cooperation and team-building.	gain a better understanding of cooperative and team-building skills.	S5: Preparing to Save; S9: Gifts of Leadership	be able to identify strengths or talents that each girl brings to group projects.
	Girls feel connected to their communities, locally and globally.	recognize the importance of being part of a larger community.	S2: "Green" Tea, Talking About Tea; Send It Home: My Water Promise; S3: Team WOW Map, Building Awareness of Water in the World; S4: LOVE, SAVE, SHARE	give examples of how group/community members help and support each other.
TAKE ACTION	**Girls are resourceful problem solvers.**	are better able to develop a basic plan to reach a goal or a solution to a problem.	S3: Rationing Water; S4: Choosing a Save Water Project; GB: P3, WOW: Teaming and Planning to Save Water	identify two or three steps and resources (people, materials, information) needed to reach a goal or solve a problem.
	Girls advocate for themselves and others.	gain a better understanding of their rights and those of others.	S1: Thinking About, Protecting Water; S3: Building Awareness of Water; S4: Planning; S7: Earning SAVE; S8: Quiet Please	name rights people have in their schools, families, or communities.
		learn and begin to apply basic advocacy skills.	S5: Communicate It!, GB: P2: WOW, p. 56	define what advocacy means and give examples of advocates in their communities.
	Girls educate and inspire others to act.	can communicate their reasons for engaging in community service and action.	S4: Heroines for Water; S7: Pass It On; S8: Educate and Inspire; GB, P1–4: All profiles of women and girls; WOWs, pp. 29, 54–57, and 85; P2: No More Heavy Lifting; P4: Beach Erosion, pp. 102–103;	explain why they chose a community action project.
	Girls feel empowered to make a difference.	increasingly feel they have important roles and responsibilities in their groups and/or communities.	GB, Part 2: Time for a WOW, pp. 26–27; Saving and Protecting Water	describe ways their actions contributed to better something (for their families, neighborhood, environment).
		exhibit increased determination to create change for themselves and others.	S6: SAVE Project; GB: P4: WOW, pp. 100–101; My WOW Awards, pp. 107–108.	give examples of when they succeeded in making positive change for themselves and others.

S=Session, GB=Girls' Book, WOW=Time for a WOW!, P=Part

From *Quest* to *WOW!*

DON'T GIVE AWAY THE MYSTERY!

If *WOW!* is the first Girl Scout leadership journey your Brownie team is embarking on, skip these "key" tips. You wouldn't want to give away the mystery of the *Brownie Quest* before the girls have a chance to uncover it on their own! Just go ahead and enjoy *WOW!*

f your Brownie Team has already enjoyed the *Brownie Quest*, keep those experiences growing by linking some of its "key" leadership ideas to the *WOW!* adventures. You might talk to the girls about how their *WOW!* experiences also put them on a trail of leadership using the three keys: **Discover** (self and values), **Connect** (team with others), and **Take Action** (to better the world). For example:

- When they consider the values of the Girl Scout Law (as on page 77 or 108 of their book), they are **Discovering**.

- When they practice team building as in the WOWs on pages 56–59 or 82–83, they are **Connecting**.

- And when they identify a way to save or protect water, carry out their plan, and go on to educate and inspire others, they are **Taking Action**.

As the Brownies pursue their *WOW!* adventures, take a moment from time to time to ask them questions that help them make the links to leadership. For example, you might ask:

- *What leadership key are we using when we look within ourselves?*

- *When we are teaming up with our Brownie group and others in the community, what leadership key are we using?*

- *How are our connections growing?*

- *When we act to save Earth, what part of leadership are we doing?*

You may find that the Brownies enjoy repeating the *Quest*'s key chants as they relate to *WOW*!

If the Brownies enjoyed going ELF, by all means ELF it up here, too!

Your Perspective on Leadership

The Girl Scout Leadership philosophy—Discover + Connect + Take Action—implies that leadership happens from the inside out. Your thoughts, enthusiasm, and approach will influence the Brownies, so take some time to reflect on your own perspective on leadership. Take a few minutes now—and throughout *WOW!*—to apply the three "keys" of leadership to yourself.

Discover	**+**	Connect	**+**	Take Action	**=**	Leadership

DISCOVER **What values do you hold related to caring for the environment? Is it ever hard to act on them? Why? What does the Girl Scout Law line "use resources wisely" mean to you?**

_____

_____

_____

CONNECT **Who would you like to add to your community network? Why do you think it's important for Brownies to connect with an expanding network of people?**

_____

_____

_____

TAKE ACTION **How does your role as a volunteer with Girl Scout Brownies contribute to making the world—and specifically the environment—better?**

_____

_____

_____

Identifying Journey "Helpers"

As on any Girl Scout journey, you don't have to do everything alone! You'll get a break and expand the girls' awareness of community by asking the family members, friends, and friends of friends to visit the Brownie Team.

So go ahead and "hand off" activities and prep steps to the Brownie Friends and Family Network. Before *WOW!* begins, aim for a brief get-together (even online!) with parents, caregivers, relatives, and friends. Find out who likes to do what, identify assistants for various *WOW!* activities, and see who has time for behind-the-scenes preparations, gathering supplies (pads, markers, glitter, glue), or "water-themed snack" duty. In some families, an aunt, older sibling, cousin, grandparent, or other adult may be most able to participate.

As part of *WOW!,* the Brownie Team will choose ideas for its SAVE and SHARE projects. It's important to let the Brownies plan their projects, but you'll find it helpful to identify contacts in the community ahead of time. Then, once the Brownie Team makes a decision, you'll have a head start on who might be able to assist their planning.

Pages 31–35 offer various letters and forms to get your Network started and to keep members informed and involved all along *WOW!*:

- Welcome Letter for the Brownie Friends and Family Network
- Sign-Up Form so that Network members can share their "skills"
- Overview of the *WOW!* Journey for Brownie Families
- Take-Home Letter for Help with *WOW!* Snacks
- Take-Home Letter for help with supplies for the Team WOW Map

REMEMBER: BROWNIES ASPIRE UP

The girls will love to spend time with older girls as they progress through *WOW.* So ask your Girl Scout council to identify a Cadette (or two!) to join *WOW.* By following the steps on the Girl Scout Cadette LiA Award letter (pages 36–37), Cadette assistants will enjoy earning an award for their leadership as they support the Brownies along their journey.

MAKING THE NETWORK WORK

Use the Brownie Friends and Family Network forms as a handy way to inform everyone of the Brownie Team's activities. The forms, which can be photocopied, (find them online at www. girlscouts.org), even note when the Brownies have a little "take home" project to do with their families. If you prefer, you can always reach out to the Network in less formal but "greener" ways—e-mail, phone, in-person chats. You might even make your own forms on reused or recycled paper.

Welcome!

Dear Brownie Friends and Family Network:

Your Brownie is sailing off on *WOW!*, a Girl Scout leadership journey all about the Wonders of Water. This experience will benefit her by guiding her to understand her own skills and values as she teams with others, learns to identify community needs, and then acts to better her community, inspiring others along the way.

On the journey, your Brownie will earn four awards that symbolize her leadership and how she is loving and protecting water!

Throughout their journey, your Brownie and her Brownie Team will need a little assistance from the Brownie Friends and Family Network! Talking to your Brownie between each session will make the experience even more beneficial to her! Just use the information provided on the attached overview to follow her experiences along *WOW*!

You will notice that after a few of the sessions, your Brownie will bring home a "Brownie Family Activity." After assisting your Brownie with the activity, be sure to send it back with her to the next session. Each activity of *WOW!* builds into the next one.

Later in the journey, the Brownies will team up on a project to save and protect water. After the girls decide what kind of project to do, we'll need help with transportation and supplies. Stay tuned for more information!

Sincerely,

_____

Brownie *WOW!* Guide
Contact Info

Phone _____

E-mail _____

Girl Scout Council (name and phone number) _____

Overview

for the Brownie Families and the Friends and Family Network

SESSION 1: LOVING WATER

_____

Date   Place   Time

The Brownies begin exploring the Wonders of Water, what they love about water, and why it's important to protect it. They will also start to create a Team WOW Map showing what they love about water. Your help in supplying colorful materials for the map is appreciated.

SESSION 2: "GREEN" TEA FOR A BLUE PLANET

_____

Date   Place   Time

Through a special tea party, the Brownies learn about the water cycle and realize that everyone on Earth shares water and that's why it's so important to save and protect it. Look for your Brownie to bring home a "water drop" that she will fill out with her water promise. She'll be asking you to join her in her promise!

SESSION 3: WATER FOR ALL

_____

Date   Place   Time

Girls report on how they carried out their promises to protect water and earn their LOVE Water awards. They then engage in activities to experience something of how families gather and use water in places where clean water is scarce. This deepens the Brownies' understanding of the need to SAVE water.

SESSION 4: TEAMING UP TO ADVOCATE FOR WATER

_____

Date   Place   Time

The Brownies create a team plan to SAVE water. Stay tuned for news about what the Brownie Team will be doing. We may need help with:

- Transportation
- Supplies
- Contacts in the community

SESSION 5: ADVOCATES COMMUNICATE!

_____

Date   Place   Time

The Brownies prepare to carry out their SAVE project as a team by practicing great communication skills. They might also learn more about their water issue through a guest visitor or even a field trip. Let us know if you can assist.

SESSION 6: SAVE!

The Brownie Team carries out its plan to speak up as advocates for water!

_____

Date   Place   Time

SESSION 7: PLANNING TO SHARE!

The Brownies discuss the success of their SAVE effort and what they learned by doing it. The girls earn their SAVE Water awards and get creative as they plan to educate and inspire even more people to get involved in protecting water. Let us know if you can assist with upcoming sessions!

_____

Date   Place   Time

SESSION 8: SHARE!

The Brownies SHARE what they have learned and how they have acted to SAVE Water with others (younger kids, family members, school community). Then they invite their guests to take action for water, too.

_____

Date   Place   Time

SESSION 9: WOW!

The Brownies reflect on their journey—from loving water as individuals to saving water as a team to sharing what they know with even more people and inviting them to protect water, too. The girls receive their _WOW!_ award. Let us know if you can help us plan the party!

_____

Date   Place   Time

Brownie Friends and Family Network

Sign-Up Form

The Brownie Team needs help. Can anyone in your family or your circle of connections provide these kinds of support?

I or someone I know can assist with:

_____ Transportation

_____ Snacks (with a "water" theme!)

_____ Meeting supplies (markers, paper, crayons, pads, markers, glitter, glue—nothing fancy; reuse and recycle as much as possible)

_____ Ideas for protecting and saving water in our community

_____ The *WOW!* Celebration

_____ Day trips

_____ Some of the Brownie meetings

Name _____

My Brownie's name _____

Phone _____

E-mail _____

Assist Your Brownie Along Her *WOW* Journey!

Dear Girl Scout Brownie Family:

Your Girl Scout Brownie is sailing off on the *WOW!* journey, a Girl Scout leadership journey all about the Wonders of Water.

To make the journey as enjoyable as possible, the Brownie Friends and Family Network is being called on to supply creative *WOW!* snacks for each Brownie gathering.

Water-themed snacks like fruits and drinks will make the best *WOW!* snacks. And several gatherings call for specific watery treats like watermelon and other fruits.

Please let us know the dates of those Brownie gatherings you can help with.

Thank you!

Assist Your Brownie with Her Team*WOW* Map!

Dear Girl Scout Brownie Family:

Your Girl Scout Brownie is sailing off on the *WOW!* journey, a Girl Scout leadership journey all about the Wonders of Water.

To get started, your Brownie will be helping to build a Team WOW Map. This map will show all the wonders of water in the lives of the Brownies.

Girls can write, draw, paint, or create collages on the map. Your assistance with creative materials will make the girls' map truly exciting.

The Brownies will appreciate any magazines, photos, crayons, colored pens and pencils, bits of fabric or foil, or any creative materials you can contribute (just remember: recycled is best!). Feel feel to let your Brownie bring these goodies to any Brownie gathering of the *WOW!* journey. Or bring them yourself. Your presence is always appreciated at Brownie gatherings.

Thank you!

Dear Girl Scout Cadette,

Just as you are *Breathe*-ing your way through a journey about air—your own and everyone else's, you've got some (actually around 800,000) little sisters who are on a journey about water—theirs—and everyone else's!

You've got air and the Brownies have water! And, of course, both are essential to life—and both are quite wondrous and awe-inspiring when you stop and appreciate them!

So, earn yourself the LiA (Leader in Action) badge by sharing some of your savvy for Earth (not to mention all of your other flairs) with a team of Brownies in your community.

Here's how:

1. Identify a team of Girl Scout Brownies on (or about to be on) their *WOW! Wonders of Water* journey. Or find a team that recently completed *WOW!* Ask your Girl Scout council for tips on how to locate a Brownie Team.

2. Talk to the volunteer guiding the Brownies and find out what the team is doing, what the Brownies enjoy, and what the volunteer finds challenging. Take a look at the Brownie *WOW* book and flip through the adult book, too!

Now the fun begins!

3. Arrange to be at some of the Brownie Team's gatherings, coordinating the schedule with the volunteers so you'll have time to do each of these:

☐ Guide the Brownies through a fun activity that teaches them something about Earth's air or water or both! You can adapt an activity from your journey for younger girls, check out some of the options in the *WOW!* girls' book and volunteer books, or create an activity of your own. A magical science experiment? Making rainbows? Making and flying a kite? Enjoy the sounds of nature? Scenty stuff? A game you invent about animals that inhabit water and sky? Or perhaps you and some friends can act out a scene from "A Very Wet ELF Adventure" or even make a short puppet show based on the story. Better yet, guide the Brownies to do their own!
Date accomplished _____

☐ Inspire the Brownies to try a new healthy habit—a watery treat (check out the ideas in the *WOW!* book), some fun cardio or yoga exercises, or a fruit or veggie grown with local water (and air!). Check with the Brownie's volunteer about food allergies before you plan any snacks. Your goal is to get the Brownies thinking about how what is good for us is often good for Earth, too!
Date accomplished _____

☐ Engage the Brownies in a short activity that gets them thinking about what great teamwork looks like. Maybe you know a game or maybe you can invent one that gets the Brownies cooperating? If not, get some ideas from other Girl Scouts in your area. Teach the game as an opening or closing or an energizing break. While the Brownies are exploring the Wonders of Water, they are also practicing another WOW—Ways of Working. Your goal is to get the Brownies practicing some really great WOWs!
Date accomplished _____

☐ Tell the Brownies a line from the Girl Scout Law that you are trying to live out in your life right now. Tell them what you are doing to bring that line to life. Then, ask them to tell you about a line they are living out!
Date accomplished _____

4. **After you've completed your mission with the Brownies,** ask the volunteer for input on what you did. What was great? What might you want to do a little differently in the future?

5. **Now that you've enjoyed some time inspiring Brownies,** think about and answer these questions:

- What did you **Discover** within yourself as you guided Brownies?

- Why it is important to **Connect** with younger girls?

- What did you accomplish on behalf of the Earth by **Taking Action** to educate and inspire Brownies?

CONGRATULATIONS! Wear your LiA with pride!

"People need to understand that their impact on water . . . affects other people around the world. We are in the same boat as people in Bangladesh . . . the Congo . . . Brazil, or the Middle East."

— Alexandra Cousteau, environmental advocate

The Journey's 9 Sample Sessions

The Sample Session plans in this guide show how to organize the *WOW!* journey into nine gatherings with girls. But if you have the time, don't rush. *WOW!* is intended to develop the girls' love for the natural world and all its wonders. So feel free to add in additional sessions, particularly if you are devoting extended time to the ELF Adventure or to camping or otherwise enjoying the great outdoors.

The group activities in the Sample Sessions elaborate on environmental and leadership themes touched on in the girls' book. So session plans will often point you to specific passages in the book that will enrich your gatherings with the girls.

It's important, though, to understand that the girls' book is meant for the Brownies' enjoyment. It is a collection of stories, creative activities, and facts meant to spark the girls' imagination and expand their knowledge of water and the world. It is something for Brownies to dip into any time they like, especially on their own, between Girl Scout gatherings. So encourage the girls to do so again and again throughout the journey. Used creatively along with the Brownies' group gatherings, the book will be something the girls treasure long after the journey ends.

The Sample Sessions include some optional activities, too. Choose those that make the most sense for your group, being alert to the interests and desires of the girls. Ask them what they would like to do!

What You'll Find in Each Session

SUGGESTIONS, NOT MUST-DO'S

If you're wondering whether you "must" do each activity or ceremony, you can usually presume the answer is no! This guide is full of suggestions for ways to give girls the Girl Scout experience of leadership. Do what's best for your Brownie Team.

At A GLANCE: The session's goal, activities, and a list of simple materials you'll need.

What to Say: Examples of what to say and ask the Brownies along the *WOW!* journey as you link activities, reflections, and learning experiences. Must you read from the "script"? Absolutely not! The girls (and you!) will have far more fun if you take the main ideas from the examples provided and then just be yourself.

Activity Instructions: Tips for guiding the girls through activities and experiences along *WOW!*, and plenty of "tools" (activity sheets, family letters, etc.) to correspond to the experiences on the journey.

Coaching to Create a Quality Experience: The quality of the Girl Scout Leadership Experience depends greatly on three processes—Girl Led, Cooperative Learning, and Learning by Doing. By following the prompts in this guide for activities, reflections, girl choice-making, and discussions, you'll be using the processes with ease.

Tying Activities to Impact: This guide notes the purpose of the journey's activities and discussions, so you'll always understand the intended benefit to girls. And you'll even be able to see the benefits—by observing the "signs" that the girls are achieving the Girl Scout National Leadership Outcomes.

WOWs: The Ways of Working role-play activities and reflections featured in the girls' book are designed to encourage and build the Brownies' leadership skills. They tie directly to the journey's leadership outcomes and offer a direct way to see the Girl Scout process of Learning by Doing in action.

Customizing the Journey

Think of these sample sessions as the main route through *WOW!*—they will get you and the girls from each step to the next, accomplishing goals along the way. As on any journey, if you and your passengers have the time, use your imagination to venture off the main route now and then to see some real-life WOWs and meet sister environmental travelers. Consider, for example:

FIELD TRIPS AND THE GREAT OUTDOORS

With assistance from the Brownie Friends and Family Network, you and the girls might visit local parks, preserves, zoos, aquariums, and botanical gardens where the girls can explore and seek out water and its many wonders. People who work at these locations will have wonderful information to share with the girls. You might also visit sites where the Brownies found their "favorite" water. All of these places give the girls a chance to explore important water issues, and will spark conversations about saving and protecting water. Outdoor adventures will not only show the girls water and water issues firsthand; they give the Brownies opportunities to deepen their love and respect for nature. So, whenever possible, invite the girls into the great outdoors. If you have access to outdoor space in the community or through your council, enjoy it as much as possible.

MAKING THINGS

Many Brownies love to create, so, depending on their interests, add a little time to a session (or add a whole session) to make a craft, try a recipe, or experiment with other projects that girls can give as gifts or enjoy themselves. And don't feel you need to do it all yourself. Ask "crafty" parents or other relatives to assist with projects related to the theme of the day's meeting. For example, perhaps some teens can assist the Brownies in making "pets" from recycled materials—in the spirit of Miwa Koizumi, featured on page 71 of the girls' book. The teens will be building leadership skills, too.

GOING ELF

If your team enjoyed the *Brownie Quest* activities involving Exploring, Linking Arms, and Flying into Action, invite girls to "Go ELF" on their *WOW!* adventures, too.

Give the ELF call whenever girls need to release a little Brownie energy.

Loving Water

This first Session introduces Brownies to the wonders of water and the importance of water in their lives.

The opening ceremony asks the girls to think about when and where they enjoy water. The subsequent discussion that you guide them through encourages them to consider why water is a precious resource and why it must be protected.

Together, these two activities open the way for the girls to begin the two steps to earning LOVE Water, their first award.

AT A GLANCE

Goal: The girls begin to express what they love about water and start to understand and experience water's importance in the world.

- Opening Ceremony: Favorite Water Activities
- Starting a Team WOW Map
- Thinking About Water Around the World
- Protecting Water: Living the Girl Scout Law
- Making Rainbows
- Send It Home: My Favorite Water
- Closing Ceremony

MATERIALS

- **Starting a Team WOW Map:** roll of butcher paper, set of poster boards, or, better yet, recycled tops or bottoms of any type of large box, or any paper or paper objects that can be pieced together to accommodate drawings, and collage items that the girls will add during each WOW gathering. Also, crayons or colored markers for writing and decorating, and assorted magazines, postcards, photos, and recycled items such as aluminum foil, cotton, blue cloth, and paper. You, the girls, and the Brownie Friends and Family Network might start a scrap box to add to and take from at each gathering.

- **Thinking About Water Around the World:** A pot of water, a small bowl of water, and a washcloth

- **Making Rainbows:** If meeting is in the daytime, a glass of water and white paper; if meeting is in the evening, a mirror, a glass of water, a shallow bowl, and a flashlight

- **Send It Home: My Favorite Water Jar:** Photocopies of take-home letter for families (page 50), or your own version on recycled paper

- **Closing Ceremony:** Cut watermelon or other melons, or an assortment of fruit.

PREPARE AHEAD

- Chat with any assistants about who will do what before and during the session.

- Set out the materials for the Team WOW Map, so the girls can easily work on it. (They will begin to decorate it with their names and favorite water activities in this session.)

- Cut up the melon or other fruit for Closing Ceremony snack.

AS GIRLS ARRIVE

Invite them to try the quiz questions in the first section of their book (pages 17, 20, and 22). Also invite them to write their names on the Team WOW Map.

Opening Ceremony: Favorite Water Activities

Invite the girls to gather in a circle and let them know they will now start this journey all about water by sharing with one another one of their favorite water activities.

You might start by naming your favorite water activity, whether it's drinking a cool glass of water on a hot day or ice-skating on a frozen pond in winter. Then invite the girls to take turns saying their favorites.

If a girl gets stuck for an answer, encourage her to think of simple, enjoyable uses of water. A girl might say, "I love to take showers," "I love to swim in the lake," or "I have the best time at the water slides." The Brownies' answers may surprise and delight you—and inspire ideas for activities and field trips all along this *WOW!* journey.

TEAM WOW MAP

The map that the girls create and refine throughout the journey will represent all the ways in which they love and protect water. Encourage the girls to add to it at each session, and to share it with guests at the journey's end.

Starting a Team WOW Map

When all the girls have shared their favorite water activities, invite them to draw or write them on the paper or poster that will be their Team WOW Map.

- Explain that this is the start of what will be their Wonders of Water or WOW "map" and they will add to it each time they gather.

- By the time the girls reach the end of their *WOW!* journey, they will have a huge creation that captures all they did together, and all the ways water is important in their lives. They will be able to share it with pride at their closing ceremony.

Encourage the girls to spread their ideas around the map with plenty of room between, so they can add more ideas each time they meet. Let them know that their map can take any form they want. What they add to it needn't follow any rigid order or time sequence.

Thinking About Water Around the World

Next, begin a discussion about how important water is to all the activities the girls talked about and drew on their map. You might say: *Those of you who said that swimming is your favorite water activity: How would you feel if there wasn't enough water to fill any pools or lakes for you to swim in?* Give the girls plenty of time to answer.

Let the girls know that the way they experience water isn't the way everyone in the world experiences water. Depending on where you live and what water resources you have, you might say something like: *In some parts of the world, people don't have a lot of water. They don't have water flowing from the faucet any time they want it.* Then ask: *Can you imagine life without clean water every day?*

Say: *Clean water is a right that every person on planet Earth has!*

Then ask: *What is a right? What are some other rights that you have?*

After the girls share some answers, sum up by saying something like: *A right is something that is necessary to have in order to live fully and be healthy and happy.*

Then say: *Now, let's experience a little of what life would be like if we did not have enough clean water!*

Ask for pairs of girls to volunteer to role-play. Explain that each pair will hear a situation in which there is less water than they are used to. They are to consider the situation and then say how they would feel if they were faced with it and what they would do. As you read the scenarios below, make them more tangible by giving the girls the appropriate props (the pot or bowl of water and washcloth). And give them plenty of time to think about the situation and present their answers.

- **Situation 1:** You only have one pot of water for all your cooking, drinking, and washing. You must share this water with your brother and sister and your mother and father. How do you feel? What would you do?

- **Situation 2:** Each day, you only have enough water for washing to wet a small cloth. That's all you have to wash yourself and anything you need to clean during the day. How do you feel? What would you do?

- **Situation 3:** You don't have enough water to keep your hands clean and brush your teeth each day. How do you feel? What would you do?

Protecting Water: Living the Girl Scout Law

Now ask the girls to turn to "The Blue Planet" section of their book (page 24). Ask for a girl to read the section to the group. After the team hears the information, which makes a good case for why water is a precious resource, ask some questions like:

- *Why do you think it's important to save water and keep it clean?*

- *How might you save water and keep it clean in your life?*

- *You have the right to water! So does everyone else in the world. What are some ways you can make sure this right to water is respected and honored for other people, too?*

Give all the girls a chance to answer. This begins their thinking about their personal water promises.

Close the conversation by asking: *If we all save water and keep it clean, what part of the Girl Scout Law are we living?* (Answer: *Using resources wisely!*) You might also ask: *In what other ways do you show that you use resources wisely?*

Now invite the girls to look at the "Loving Water" section of their book (page 29), which asks them to list ways they can help care for water, such as stopping dripping faucets and wasted water running down a drain.

- Ask the girls to think about the list between now and their next gathering. Their goal is to look for all the places they see water in their life and note how it could be treated better. At their next gathering, they will share all their ideas for treating water better.

BROWNIE DISCUSSIONS & REFLECTIONS

Engaging girls in discussions about the importance of water in their daily life helps them reflect on what they experience in their Brownie gathering and apply it to their own lives. Discussions and reflections are an important part of the Learning by Doing cycle, a learning process that makes Girl Scouting unique. So keep that Brownie chatter flowing! It's truly a purposeful experience.

Making Rainbows

To introduce this unique phenomenon of light and water, invite the girls to describe any rainbows they have seen. You might say: *Do you remember a time when you saw a rainbow? What was the weather like?*

As each girl tells her story, guide the group to see what their stories have in common. You might ask: *Is there anything that all these rainbow stories have? Is it something that we have been talking a lot about?* (Answer: *Water! And light! Rainbow stories all have water and light, even if the water comes from a garden hose or sits in a puddle and the light comes from a flashlight.*)

Next, explain that there are ways to make a rainbow indoors, too, and that's what they're about to do!

Method 1: If your meeting room gets sunlight

- Fill a glass or glass vase with water. Place the glass on a table in front of a sunny window.
- Invite one of the girls to place a sheet of white paper on the floor in front of the table and window.
- Ask the girls to arrange themselves on both sides of the paper without blocking the light from the window.
- If no rainbow appears, invite two girls to assist you in adjusting the glass and paper until a rainbow is visible.

Method 2: If your meeting room has white walls and can be darkened

- Place a mirror inside a full glass of water.
- Place the glass either on the floor or on a low table.
- Ask the girls to stand around the glass.
- Invite them to take turns shining a flashlight into the water, moving it around until a rainbow can be viewed.

RAINBOWS 3 WAYS

Offered here are three variations for making rainbows indoors. Choose the one that works best with your setting. Can you count on sunshine coming through a window? Can you create a completely dark room? If these are not possible, choose Method 3, which lets you create a rainbow with just a shallow pan, a mirror, and a flashlight.

Method 3:

- Fill a shallow pan with water until it is three-quarters full.

- Place a mirror at the pan's edge.

- Invite each girl to shine the flashlight directly into the mirror, while another girl positions a sheet of white paper so the reflection of the light shines on it. You might say: *Now move this piece of white paper until it "captures" the light. (You may also need to adjust the mirror until the girls can see the watery reflection on the paper.)*

- Invite the girls to look closely at the edge of the reflection and describe what they see. (They should be able to see all the colors of the rainbow.)

TALKING ABOUT RAINBOWS

As the girls marvel at the rainbow you've created together, invite them to explain what is happening. You might remind them that rainbows are explained on page 11 of their book.

As a handy reference, here's the science behind rainbows: When light travels in a straight line it is known as white, or clear, light. When light is bent by water or water vapor, it breaks into the seven colors of a rainbow. The colors always appear in the same order: red, orange, yellow, green, blue, indigo, and violet.

- Invite each girl to name the colors of the rainbow, to note the order in which they appear, and to share her favorite color of the rainbow.

- When each has had her say, you might note if any colors were left out. If so, ask the girls to try to name the missing colors. You might walk them through Roy G. Biv, a fun "name" for remembering all the colors.

- Remind the girls of the rainbow Jamila, Alejandra, and Campbell see in the ELF Adventure. You might ask: *Do you remember the colors of the girls' slickers?* If any girls in your group have taken the *Brownie Quest* or the *Welcome to the Daisy Flower Garden* journey, you might ask: *Can anyone figure out why Campbell wears a red slicker?* (Answer: *She likes the color red, and she likes tomatoes!*)

- Ask: *Have you ever made a rainbow before? What did you learn today? How does it feel to learn something new? Now that you know how to make a rainbow, who might you teach to make a rainbow?*

Send It Home: My Favorite Water

Explain to the girls that they will start their next gathering with a special ceremony: sharing their favorite water. Invite each girl to find a special jar and fill it with water from a favorite water source—a lake, a stream, a backyard pond, a kitchen faucet, an aquarium, even a hose. Each girl will bring her sealed (with a tight lid!) jar of favorite water to the next session and tell the group about where her water came from and what makes it special. Give each girl a copy of the Take-Home Letter about the Water Jar activity (available for photocopying on page 50, or make your own "greener" versions).

Also, invite the girls to think about all the places they might find water in their community and to have fun with the My Own Wonders of Water page in their book (pages 30–31). Encourage them to let you know what they might like to do on this journey. You might say: *What activities or ideas would you like to explore when we get together? When something comes to mind, let me know!*

Closing Ceremony

Invite the girls into a circle and explain that they are going to end this Brownie gathering by sampling a water-filled food. Bring out the plate of cut fruit and ask the girls to each take a piece, guess how much of it is water, and say one wish they have for the world's water, and then pass the plate to the next girl.

When all the girls have selected a piece of fruit, guessed how much water is in it, and made a water wish, it's time to take a bite and enjoy! If the girls are eating watermelon, let them know that it is 92 percent water. You might explain in a simple way what percent means: *A portion of a whole, with the whole being 100. So 92 percent is a lot of water!* (If serving other fruits, here's a rundown of the water content of some popular fruits: apples, 84 percent; bananas, 74 percent; cantaloupe, 90 percent; grapes, 81 percent; oranges, 87 percent; pineapple, 87 percent; strawberries, 92 percent.)

Let the girls know that throughout this journey they will learn more fun facts about water and all the places it shows up in the world. You might point out the colorful map, A World That's Wet and Dry, on pages 26–27 of their book.

Assist Your Brownie with Her *WOW!* Water Jar

Dear Girl Scout Brownie Family:

Your Girl Scout Brownie is sailing along on the *WOW!* journey, a Girl Scout leadership journey all about the Wonders of Water.

To deepen your Brownie's LOVE for water, she has been asked to select a special water jar, fill it with water from her favorite water source, and bring it to our next Brownie gathering.

Please help your Brownie be ready to share her favorite water at our next session, where she'll also have a chance to decorate her jar. If you and she have some special decorations fitting of a water jar, invite your Brownie to bring them to our next gathering, too. The more goodies the Brownies bring, the more variety there will be to share with the full Brownie Team.

Thank you!

Assist Your Brownie with Her Water Drops

Dear Girl Scout Brownie Family:

As your Girl Scout Brownie continues to sail through *WOW!*, a Girl Scout leadership journey all about the Wonders of Water, she's going to call on you for your support and advice.

Today she's bringing home some water drops. These will be used to symbolically hold the water promises she makes and carries out.

She's going to ask you to join in with her on her water promise. She'll be sharing her promise and your efforts to join in with her at our next Brownie gathering.

Thank you!

PHOTOCOPY THESE WATER DROPS FOR THE GIRLS TO USE AS NEEDED. OR, BETTER YET, INVITE THE GIRLS TO HAVE SOME FUN MAKING THEIR OWN WATER DROPS ON RECYCLED SCRAP PAPER!

"Green" Tea for a Blue Planet

AT A GLANCE

Goal: As girls continue to explore what they love about water, they expand their knowledge of the water cycle and consider what promise they'll make to protect water.

- Opening Ceremony: Our Favorite Water Places

- Team WOW Map

- "Green" Tea for a Blue Planet (or States of Water Stations)

- Loving and Protecting Water: Continuing the Conversation

- Send It Home: My Water Promise

- Closing Ceremony: The Water Cycle

MATERIALS

- **Rainbow-Making:** a glass of water and white paper (the same materials used in Session 1) to give girls the opportunity to enjoy some rainbows as they arrive

- **Our Favorite Water Places:** a selection of jars or other containers suitable for holding water (enough to have one each for any girls who might have forgotten or not been able to find one), labels, stickers, felt pens, paints, glitter, etc.

- **"Green" Tea for a Blue Planet:** electric teakettle, hot plate, or microwave; heatproof cups (one for each girl); ice cubes (at least three for each girl); assorted tea bags (one for each girl); a bag, cup, or other receptacle for collecting used tea bags; large spoon or tongs; optional: juice and sparkling water (enough to make each cup of tea more "girl friendly," if desired); a "watery" snack, such as watermelon or pineapple chunks

- **States of Water Stations** (if not doing "Green" Tea for a Blue Planet): water, electric teakettle or hot plate, aluminum foil, freezer or small cooler filled with ice or ice bricks

- **"Water Drops"** and explanatory Take-Home Letter for girls to bring home (photocopy from pages 50–51, or your own verson on recycled paper)

PREPARE AHEAD

- Look over pages 15 and 72–73 of the girls' book to familiarize yourself with the water cycle and some interesting facts about tea and Girl Scouts.

- Chat with any assistants about their roles before and during the session.

- Set up the "Green Tea" or State of Water materials. The Brownie Friends and Family Network might be able to help supply them.

- Photocopy the Take-Home "Water Drop" letter, and the water drops (pages 50-51), which the girls will bring back to the next gathering.

- Have the Team WOW Map and assorted materials ready for the girls to work with.

- Write the closing poem (page 61) on a big piece of paper or poster board so the girls can say it together.

AS GIRLS ARRIVE

Invite them to set up the materials for the "Green" Tea for a Blue Planet or the States of Water activity station(s) and the WOW map. They might also like to make some rainbows!

Opening Ceremony: Our Favorite Water Places

Invite the girls into a circle with their jars of water from their favorite water places. Encourage any girl who forgot her jar or doesn't have one yet to join the circle as well.

Ask each girl to describe the place where she collected her water and what she liked about that water source. You might prompt each girl to describe some specifics about the water. Ask: *Is this freshwater or saltwater? Is it clean enough to drink?*

The girls' answers will serve to remind them of water places in their region. Any girls who didn't fill a jar might say where they plan to collect their water. Remember: The source of the water can be a tap or hose; it doesn't need to be a natural place such as a pond or rainfall. You might say: *Your* WOW! *journey will cover all kinds of water on the planet we share.*

Next, bring out the art supplies and invite the girls to decorate their water jars in any way they like, using the materials you and they, and perhaps the Brownie Friends and Family Network, brought to the gathering.

- Begin by saying something like: *Remember to give the lid of your jar an extra twist so nothing spills. Each drop is precious!*

- Then suggest that each girl label her jar with her name, the place she found the water, and the date she collected it. Adhesive labels or small pieces of paper can be used.

- Then invite each girl to decorate the jar in any way she likes. You might suggest that she start with scenes of her favorite water place.

Team WOW Map

- Now invite the girls to add their special water places to their Team WOW Map. Encourage them to add any other items to the map that show what they love or know about water.

"Green" Tea for a Blue Planet

Having a tea party that begins with hot tea and ends with iced tea is a festive way for the girls to see what the Brownie friends experienced in the first chapter of their water adventure: that as water travels through the water cycle, it takes on many forms—from liquid to vapor to solid. The girls will gain a basic understanding of three states of water: precipitation, condensation, and evaporation.

And by drinking their tea after learning all the science involved, the Brownies won't waste a drop of water. So they are having a "green" tea, even if the tea they drink isn't green but red or yellow or orange! Let them know that "green" isn't just a color; it also means being good to the environment. You might also remind the girls that by not wasting any water, they're using resources wisely—and that's living the Girl Scout Law!

TALKING ABOUT TEA

Before you heat the water for tea, take a few minutes to talk to the girls about how many people around the world use tea—and how they use it in different ways. You might let them know that:

- Tea is grown in countries as diverse as China, Kenya, Turkey, and Argentina. Do the girls know which continents those countries are on?

- Mostly tea is used as a drink, but some people dye cloth with it, too. And although some people drink it every day in a casual way, others drink it in ceremonies that follow special rules.

- Juliette Gordon Low, the founder of Girl Scouts, liked to drink tea, and in the ELF Adventure, Grandma Elf also enjoys tea. Let the girls know that pages 72–73 of their book have lots of fun facts about tea.

Explain that tea is one very big way that water unites people around the world.

Next, steer the conversation to how the girls might see tea being used in their own lives. Ask: *Who in your family drinks tea? At what time of day do they drink it? What kinds of tea do they drink? What kinds have you tried?*

The girls might also enjoy knowing about bubble tea. If the girls haven't heard of it, let them know that it's a cold drink made with tea and tapioca that started about 20 years ago, in Taiwan. You might say: *Sometimes the pearls of tapioca are so big that bubble tea is drunk with a very fat straw—otherwise the tapioca would get stuck and block the tea from coming through!*

CYCLING THROUGH THE WATER CYCLE

Depending on the size of your group, your meeting room, and available assistance from other adult volunteers, the tea party can be one big event or a few smaller parties.

If you opt to create water stations instead, you can set up one station or a series of stations that the girls can visit in smaller groups. By staggering their starting times and places, each group can enter the water cycle at a different spot. Encourage the girls to use what they learn to understand the Water Cycle pictured on page 15 of their *WOW!* book.

LET THE TEA PARTY BEGIN!

- Heat water for the tea. If you have access to a sink, ask each girl to wash her hands—without wasting water! Use the opportunity to remind the girls about water's role in good hygiene, as discussed in Session 1.

- Next, invite each girl to choose a tea bag and a cup, and to gather around the kettle (or whatever device you are using to heat the water).

- Explain that heating water is a quick way to demonstrate the change of water from liquid to vapor, which is called evaporation.

- Remind the girls that liquid water is always evaporating, and condensing, just not as quickly or completely as when water is heated. While the water is heating, remind the girls that in the ELF Adventure, the Brownie friends watch a sparkly water drop evaporate as part of the never-ending water cycle.

- As the water heats, you might also add a little spelling lesson. You might say: *Let's all say—and then spell—the word evaporation.*

- Invite the girls to think of other examples of liquid water turning to vapor (as when using a humidifier in winter). If the girls wish to know more about hot vapor, here's the science behind it: Molecules that make up water take in energy from the heat source and begin moving so fast they "bounce" away or escape from the liquid as steam.

- When the water is boiling, pour some into each girl's cup so that it is filled halfway. The girls should be able to see vapor rising as their tea brews.

- After a few minutes (or the amount of time required to create a slightly darker tea than normal), ask the girls to remove their tea bags. Invite one girl to collect them safely and neatly. Let the girls know that rather than throwing tea bags into the garbage, they can be added to compost so they can help a garden grow. You might ask: *Does anyone have a compost heap at home where we could put the tea bags? And: If you let tea bags help a garden instead of just landing in the garbage, what line of the Girl Scout Law are you living?* (Answer: *Using resources wisely!*)

FROM HOT TO COLD, AND VAPOR TO SOLID

- Next, break out your stash of ice cubes and distribute one to each girl, using a spoon or tongs. Explain that ice is water in a solid state—so, with their tea, they have now experienced water as vapor, liquid, and a solid! Ask each girl to put the ice cube into her tea. You might ask: *What's happening? Is the solid water, the ice cube, becoming something else?* (Answer: *It's melting into a liquid—the state it started in!*)

- Give each girl a second ice cube and ask her to place it in her cup. If the ice melts quickly, distribute a third round of ice cubes.

- Pass ice cubes to the girls until each cup of tea has changed from hot tea to iced tea with an ice cube floating in it. (The ice cubes float because they are lighter than the liquid water.) Soon the girls should see water droplets forming on the outside of their cups. Explain that this process is called condensation, and it's what the Brownie friends learned from Brownie Elf in the ELF Adventure. Invite the girls to chant the word *condensation* together, just as the friends did in the story.

- Explain that the condensation on their cups will soon drip down as liquid water—the very thing that started all their tea-making in the first place!

Now invite the girls to take a sip of tea (first, add any special extras your group has chosen, such as fruit juice or sparkling water) and enjoy their drink with another water-filled snack—fruit! Ask the girls to consider that around the world, people are drinking tea or some other water-based beverage, right along with them! You might say: *No matter how we like our tea—hot or cold, red or green, sweet or bitter—the sips we take today are a special way of showing how water unites all of us, all around the world.*

GO GLOBAL!

As the girls sip, they might like to toast each other in a variety of languages. Cheers! *Salud! L'chaim!*

Option: States of Water Stations

Step 1: To show water turning from liquid to vapor, heat water in an electric teakettle or on a hot plate until steam is visible.

Step 2: Using a pot holder, move an object cooler than the heated water— such as a glass, a mirror, or a plate—close to the stream of vapor. As the vapor hits the cooler object, it will form back into water droplets, just as water vapor in clouds becomes liquid again as rain.

- Pass the object around so the girls can see the droplets up close.

- Explain that this process is called condensation, and it's what the Brownie friends learned from Brownie Elf in the ELF Adventure. Invite the girls to chant the word *condensation* together, just as the Brownie friends did in the ELF Adventure.

- Remind the girls that a drop of water can travel all over the world. You might say: *Water, like air, is something all people SHARE; what each of you does to water can affect other girls far away.*

- Invite the girls to see how eventually enough water droplets form on the cooler object that the droplets begin running off it—just as rain falls from clouds. Explain to the girls that water drops falling from clouds fill rivers and lakes, and seep into the ground, or, when there's water left over, become runoff.

- Invite a girl to hold a folded piece of aluminum foil to serve as a riverbed to catch the water droplets.

Step 3: If your meeting room has a kitchen with a freezer, fill ice cube trays or several small containers with water. If you don't have access to a freezer, place the trays or containers in a cooler lined with ice or freezer bricks.

- Ask the girls to place the trays in the freezer (or cooler) and to guess how long it will take for water to transform into its third possible state—a solid, ice.

Before the session ends, check to see whether the water is becoming solid. If it's not, leave it and invite the girls to view it again at their next gathering.

SKIP THE TEA, BUT STILL LEARN ALL ABOUT WATER!

If a tea party doesn't excite the girls or you, opt for this more straightforward look at the states of water.

During Step 1, use the same discussion points given in the third through sixth bullet points under "Green" Tea for a Blue Planet on page 56.

Loving and Protecting Water: Continuing the Conversation

Now that girls have plunged into the world of water, they can probably talk at length about what they know and love about it. Their discussion will guide them further along in the steps toward their LOVE Water award, which they can earn in Session 3.

- Start a discussion by saying something like: *Think about all the reasons you LOVE water. Do you have some special reasons for loving water? What are they?* Encourage the girls to think carefully. Let them know that the next time they gather, each girl will name her top two reasons for loving water and write them in her book as a step to the LOVE Water award.

- Guide the conversation to ways to protect water. Start by asking: *What do you know about water that you didn't know before today? How do you feel when you learn something new?*

Then ask the girls what ideas they have for their Loving Water lists, which they started thinking about in Session 1. Remind them that the list is on page 29 of their book. You might ask: *Where in your life did you find places to treat water better? What might you now want to tell people about water so that they, too, will treat it well?*

Check out the definition of "Advocate" on page 56 of the girls' book with them. Let them know that each time they speak up to encourage others to treat Earth well, they are being advocates! That's important! Let the Brownies know that as they work toward their SAVE Water award, they'll have a chance to speak up and be advocates for water.

As the discussion continues, encourage the girls to think of their sharing of ideas as a way of pooling all their water drops. You might say: *Soon you will have enough ideas that you'll be able to fill a bucket with water drops!* Then say: *At the end of Brownie gathering today, you will promise to change one personal practice in your life so that you will help save water or keep it clean. And you'll invite your family to join you. So let's start thinking about what you might do—we'll get a head start!*

Explain to the girls that saving water at home and protecting water are the two big ideas to think about. Ask: *What personal promises can you make that would help save or protect water?*

BROWNIES HAVE MANY WAYS TO ADVOCATE!

Take a few moments to let girls know that they can be advocates for people, too! You can even invite them to brainstorm a list of ways that they can speak up to make sure other people are treated well. Then, as the WOW journey continues, encourage them to check their list. How are they acting as advocates?

- Next, talk with the girls about how important it is to choose a promise they can stick to. You might say: *Choosing your water promise is a way that you can live the Girl Scout Law. Does anyone know which line of the Law is about sticking to your promises?* (The answer: *Responsible for what I say and do.*) Encourage the girls to think about how a promise doesn't have to be big to be important. In fact, you might ask if they want to agree as a team to make "less is more" types of promises: Each girl will agree to do something small, personally and within her family, because even though it is small, it is still important.

- Then ask: *When you make a promise, you are giving yourself a new challenge. What do you think a challenge is? Why are challenges good?*

- After girls share their ideas, you can sum up by saying something like: *When we take on a new challenge we open ourselves up to try new things and learn new skills. It's great to learn new things, especially when it means stretching yourself a little. That's how you grow—as a person and as a leader! So, when you make a promise for water, make one that you know you can do—but that gives you a little challenge, too!*

- Guide the girls to think about the exact promise each wants to make. Encourage each girl to choose her own promise, one that works best for her as an individual.

Page 54–55 of the girls' book contains several Ways of Working tips that encourage positive talk and action. Ask the girls to share any additional tips of their own, and encourage them to write those tips in their book. If time permits, invite the girls to pair up and then use the tips to role-play how they will talk to their families about their promises. Girls can take turns being themselves and a family member.

The three most important things the girls must say are:

- What the water problem is

- Why it matters to them and why it should matter to their family

- How they can help solve the problem

Send It Home: My Water Promise

Invite the girls to talk with their families about the water promise they would like to make. Give each girl a "water drop" (or a few!) and ask them to use a water drop to "capture" the water promise they agree on after talking with their families. Encourage the girls to use their WOW talking points to inspire their families to make the promise, too. Let the girls know that they will start their next gathering by reporting back on how they have fulfilled their water promise. So they should all bring back their water drops with their promise written on it.

Closing Ceremony: The Water Cycle

Invite the girls to form a Friendship Circle and explain that they are going to end this Brownie gathering by imitating the water cycle. Ask the girls to join hands and walk slowly in one direction, then stop and walk slowly in the other direction. Remind them that this is what the water cycle does—it's a never-ending circle of movement from one state of water to another.

Now invite the girls to create their own chant—or rap—to say as they move. You could also suggest this one, which you might write on a large sheet of paper or poster board:

> *Water, water, here and there*
> *We are Brownies and we care*
> *Liquid flows and vapor rises*
> *Snowflakes drift, ice disguises*
> *Water changes round and round*
> *Brownies watch the rain fall down.*

Suggest a simple gesture for one of the verbs (for example, fingers jiggling and floating upward for "vapor rises"). Then invite the girls to "choreograph" a gesture for each verb; if this happens, you'll have a little moving dance. The girls are likely to have fun falling down for "watch the rain fall down."

Water for All

AT A GLANCE

Goal: Girls select their top two reasons for loving water and earn the LOVE Water award after they report back on how they carried out their promise. They also deepen their understanding of why it's so important that people's right to water is respected and honored around the world through access to clean water.

- Opening Ceremony: Loving Water
- Team WOW Map
- Building Awareness of Water in the World
- Closing Ceremony

MATERIALS

- **Extra water drops:** for any girls who didn't bring theirs
- **Team WOW Map:** Colored pencils, markers, glue, and any other supplies for the girls to continue building their map
- **Gathering Water:** Cloth strips, lightweight bundles, two reusable cups for each girl, and three coolers (one with muddy water, one empty, one with clean water), or your own choice of materials to make the activity come alive for the girls (See activity steps, pages 65–66.)
- **Rationing Water:** A bucket of water, a small doll, small pans and cloths, or any other materials needed to bring the activity to life for the girls (See activity steps, page 66–67.)
- LOVE Water awards

PREPARE AHEAD

- If you know girls or families from places where water is scarce, invite them to share in planning and doing the session activities. To enliven the gathering, answer questions, and guide the girls, you and the Brownies might also locate and invite immigrants or refugees from drought-stricken areas of the world, or from areas with little or no running water.

- You might also invite an international aid worker or a former Peace Corps volunteer. If possible, decorate the meeting room with pictures from the country in which your guests lived or worked, or with images of wells, springs, and rivers from which women and girls around the world gather water.

- Set up the Gathering Water stations before the Brownies arrive. If possible, do the activity outdoors—weather is a factor for water gatherers.

AS GIRLS ARRIVE

Ask if they filled in a water drop with how they've chosen to protect water. If not, they can do it now. Girls might also like to decorate their water drops or add an image of their efforts to the Team WOW Map.

Opening Ceremony: Loving Water

Invite the girls into a Friendship Circle. Distribute a small clear glass filled with drinking water to each girl. Invite them, one by one, to come to the middle of the circle and state two reasons they LOVE water and the water promise they have carried out. Ask each girl: *Did you take a positive risk and learn something new? What?*

After each girl has taken a turn, reinforce the girls' commitments by saying:

- *We have learned to LOVE water and understand the water cycle.*
- *We have all promised to care about water.*
- *Now toast yourselves and your LOVE Water award, and drink up!*

While the girls toast one another and drink their water, hand out the LOVE Water awards.

The girls may want to invent their own chant or rap to close this special ceremony. Or they might recite this one:

Water, water here and there
We are Brownies and we care
We mapped our world and pledged for sure
To do one thing to keep it pure.

Then collect all the water drops representing the water that the girls have protected and saved. Keep the drops in a special jar or bucket. You'll use them in Session 4.

Team WOW Map

Invite the girls to add some more water wonders to their Team WOW Map. You might want to guide them to see how some water places—like a town reservoir, for example—provide water for all of them. Or how hurting water in one place—such as throwing trash into a lake or an ocean—hurts the water for all of them. Emphasize that the girls share the same water, and that's why it's important to care for water everywhere.

Encourage the girls to add anything they like to the map that will help represent water in their world. They might bring in photos from newspapers and magazines, make their own drawings, or use stickers.

Remind them that the map is a journey-long project and they can add to it or edit out places and images as they go. By revising the map and enhancing its appeal, they will create a WOW map that truly wows them all!

KEEPING THE PROMISE

As they travel through the journey, encourage the girls to remind themselves of their water promises.

At later gatherings, you might do a "check-up." Invite the girls to report on what they did to love water that week, whether it was something they promised or something new.

Building Awareness of Water in the World

The following two water-gathering activities deepen the Brownies' awareness of water in the world.

Start by talking with the girls about how clean water is essential for life, but not everyone in the world has easy access to clean water. If you and the girls invited any guests, invite them to join the discussion.

Guide the girls toward an understanding of how, in some parts of the world, water is scarce and difficult to gather—it doesn't just flow out of a tap! Ask: *Do you remember what an advocate is? What does an advocate do? (Answer: Speak up for the rights of others and Earth, too.) Everyone has the right to water. Let's explore what happens if you don't have enough water.*

GATHERING WATER

Now it's time for the girls to experience some of the effort and time it takes to find and carry fresh water.

Ask the girls if they've read "A Wide World of Water Vessels" and "No More Heavy Lifting" on pages 49–50 in their book. If they haven't, invite them to take turns reading those sections out aloud. Then, explain to them how it is often a girl's job to fetch water throughout the day, even if it means walking for miles while carrying a younger brother or sister. Explain that the cups they will use today symbolize the large containers or buckets that some girls carry, containers that may hold many gallons of water. Then get started:

- Ask the girls to use the strips of cloth to tie a bundle on one another to represent a younger sibling who must be carried. Assist them as needed.

- Then invite each girl to take two cups and set off, one by one, along the obstacle course, to find clean drinking water.

- Encourage the girls to use their imagination as they walk. You might say: *Imagine the hot sun beating down on your head, and your little brother or sister crying and fussing.*

- When the girls reach the first station, they find muddy water with debris in it. Ask: *Why can't you drink this? What would happen if you did?*

LEARNING ABOUT SAVING WATER

Role-playing the difficulties of gathering water in regions where water is scarce helps the girls appreciate how important it is to conserve water. It's a reminder that even though we live on the Blue Planet, there is not much fresh water on Earth and we all have to share it.

EXPANDING THEIR
VIEW OF THE WORLD

If the Brownies understand
the struggles of others,
they will be better able to
look critically at all sorts of
issues they may face—and
they will be less likely to
waste water.

- At the second station, girls find an empty cooler—the well or river is dry. Ask: *Why might the well be dry? What does this mean for your family?*

- At the third station, girls find a full cooler with clean water, but the line waiting for it may be long. The water flow might be weak, which means it takes longer to pump. It could take hours to fill large buckets.

- Invite each girl to walk back holding one cup of water on her head and one by her side. Remind the water carriers that every drop is precious and they can't spill or slosh along the way.

When all the girls have returned, invite them to sit in a Friendship Circle with their cups. Ask: *What was the hardest thing about transporting your two cups of water?* Then ask: *How did you feel at each station? Were you frustrated? Angry? Happy? If girls are in charge of getting water, what opportunities are they missing? School? Other forms of learning? Play? If they miss school, what does that mean for their future?*

Encourage the girls to visit a library to learn about a country with scarce water resources. Encourage them to report back on the similarities and differences they find between their own community and life in a country where water is scarce.

RATIONING WATER

Open a discussion about all the daily activities that require water. You might say: *Begin in the morning: Do you take a shower? Brush your teeth? Now think about how much water you and your family might need throughout a whole day.*

LEARNING TO
RATION WATER

Now that the girls have
experienced some of the
difficulties of gathering
water in a region where
water is scarce, they
will team up to role-play
rationing a set amount of
water for a day's tasks.

Next, ask the girls to imagine dividing up the small amount of water brought home in their bucket to do all the jobs they've just named. You might ask: *Would there be enough water? Why or why not? How could you make the water last longer?*

Let the girls know that they will now work together to decide how to use one bucket of water to complete four tasks: cooking oatmeal, washing dishes, bathing a baby, and doing laundry. Ask the girls to divide into groups of three or four and go to one of the areas where you have set out a bucket of water, a small doll, and some miniature towels and pans. Ask the girls to determine how much water each task needs. You might ask: *Which task will need the most water? Which the least?*

Ask the girls to decide the order in which they should do the tasks. You might say: *Consider which tasks need clean water and which tasks could use the same water. How about water for drinking? Is there enough?*

After the girls have decided on the order of the tasks, invite them to reflect on their decisions. You might ask each group: *Did you have enough water for all the tasks? If not, how did you decide which tasks were most important? Were you able to find a strategy for using the water in the wisest way?*

Close the discussion by guiding the girls to understand that water is so scarce in some places that each day millions of women and children have to make the kind of hard choices they just did in their Brownie gathering. Say: *That's why it's so important for you to learn to protect Earth's water—and advocate for everyone to have the right to enough clear water.*

Closing Ceremony

Gather the Brownies in a circle and discuss what they have learned about water around the world.

Bring a container or cup of water to the circle. Invite the girls to carefully pass the container from one to another. You might want to say: *Let's remember that fresh water is scarce and try not to spill any. If you do, it's OK. But let's slow down and try not to.* The girls might enjoy it if you encourage them to sing/chant:

> *Careful, careful with each drop!*
> *There is no more, so waste must stop!*

Let the girls know that at the next gathering they will, as a team, come up with an idea to protect Earth's water. By keeping water clean and not wasting it, they can contribute to solving the water problems around the world. P.S. Use the water you passed around to refresh a nearby plant!

RAISING AWARENESS

As the girls make choices about how to ration water, they expand their awareness of global water issues.

Teaming Up as Advocates to SAVE Water

AT A GLANCE

Goal: The Brownies take on a challenge of saving water as they decide on the best idea for a team project and then create a plan that allows them to advocate for water and for the right of all to this precious resource.

- Opening Ceremony: Heroines for Water

- LOVE, SAVE, SHARE

- Creating a SAVE Project

- Closing Ceremony: Capturing the SAVE Vision on the Team's WOW Map

MATERIALS

- Photocopies, double-sided if possible, of the "LOVE, SAVE, SHARE" story and the empty WOW! story panels (pages 72–73)

- Large paper or poster board for planning
- Team WOW Map

PREPARE AHEAD

- Flip through the *WOW!* book and read the various stories about what women and girls are doing to love and save water around the world. Make note of those that you find most inspirational.

AS GIRLS ARRIVE

Invite them to add images of people around the world gathering and rationing water to their Team WOW Map. They might also like to look at the "Save and Share" examples in their books on pages 56–59.

Opening Ceremony: Heroines for Water

Bring the girls together and ask them to flip through their *WOW!* books to check out all the examples of girls and women who are loving and saving Earth's water. Ask: *Do you have a favorite? Who is it? Why?* Remind the girls that they have something in common with these heroines: They're acting to SAVE water, too! You might let the girls know which profiles inspire you the most and why.

Ask: *Among all these women and girls, can you find examples of ways that they are being advocates who speak up on behalf of others? What examples of positive risk-taking can you find? When these people made mistakes, what did they learn from them?*

LOVE, SAVE, SHARE

Give the girls copies of the illustrated "LOVE, SAVE, SHARE" story on page 72–73.

- Have the team read the short story together—or even act it out.

- Compare what is happening in the story to the way water travels from a small stream to a river and, eventually, to the ocean.

- Invite the girls to create their own last few panels of the story and to take turns sharing their endings. Encourage them to include ideas about how the characters can take positive risks and also be advocates. Then invite the girls to use the WOW! page of empty panels to create a story of their own team's SAVE and SHARE efforts in the full page of panels.

- Ask: *Why is it more powerful for a lot of people to act together for water instead of one person acting alone?*

GET CREATIVE

If the girls are interested, how about making the team story into a large mural? Or they might create it on a computer or act it out as a skit.

A GREAT SAVE PROJECT

- Relies on girl input in choosing and planning it

- Gives girls the opportunity to work as a team

- Enables girls to advocate for water by talking to others and educating and inspiring them

PROJECT EXAMPLES

- Work with a school library or other community building to place signs by faucets warning people not to waste water

- Host a family meeting to ask all families to reduce or eliminate bottled water

- Make a booklet, play, or other creative endeavor to offer tips for protecting water to other girls, families, or schools

- Something else based on the girls' imagination!

Choosing a SAVE Project

Start a discussion with the girls about how they will now reach out into their community just as Jamila, Campbell, and Alejandra did in the "LOVE, SAVE, SHARE" story. You might say:

- *You've each been showing you LOVE water by protecting it on your own.*

- *Now we're going to join forces as a Brownie Team and plan a SAVE project that will protect even more of Earth's water.*

Spread out all the water drops that girls have filled in, showing how they have individually cared for water. Also spread out their Team WOW Map.

Ask: *What ideas do you have for a SAVE project that we could do as a team?*

As girls share ideas, encourage them to think about challenging themselves, by asking questions like:

- *Which of these project ideas will be a fun, new challenge for you?*

- *What could you learn from it?*

- *Would it give you a chance to take a positive risk?*

Ask for a girl volunteer to list all the ideas, coaching her as needed. Besides looking at their water drops, the Brownies can review the ideas on pages 56–59 of their book ("Saving and Protecting Water"). You might ask:

- *Where are all the places people use water? How could we use less?*

- *Have you noticed a lot of people drinking from plastic water bottles? How does that impact Earth's water? What could we do instead that would be better for Earth?*

Once the list is done, ask the girls if there are any ideas that, while interesting, may just not be doable for the group. Point out any that you know won't be realistic, too!

- Ask the Brownies which SAVE project idea they are most interested in doing together. Encourage them to say why, too.

- When all the girls have had a chance to talk, see if one idea has risen to the top. If not, you might hold a team vote.

• Wrap up by mentioning that on a team, sometimes members compromise—that means they show some give and take—so they can move forward together. Once a decision is made about which project to do, check for any bruised feelings if the decision did not go someone's way. Then congratulate the girls for compromising in order to reach a team decision.

PLANNING THE PROJECT

A simple planning worksheet, like the one below, might help the girls move their project plan forward. Depending on the girls' project, the ideas offered in the "Saving and Protecting Water" section of the girls' book (pages 56–59) might help them answer the questions in the worksheet.

Our SAVE idea is _____.

This project allows us to be advocates for water because _____
_____.

We will be talking to _____ about _____
_____.

What we will do _____

Supplies we need _____

This project will be a new challenge for us because we will be taking a positive risk to _____.

We hope we learn _____.

What each member of the team will do:

     Name _____ Action _____

     Name _____ Action _____

Closing Ceremony: Capturing the SAVE Vision on the Team's WOW Map

Ask the girls to gather around their Team WOW Map to add their vision of their SAVE project to it. Guide them to cover the key aspects of the plan by asking: *What will the result of your SAVE effort be? What will it do for water?* Then congratulate the Brownies on their SAVE effort!

RECORDING THEIR SAVE PROJECT IDEA

You might also remind the Brownies that they can fill in their SAVE project information on page 83 of their book.

WOW! LOVE, SAVE, SHARE!

Jamila learns that she can wash her hands and brush her teeth without running sooo much water! She **LOVES** water, so she shuts the faucet off.

Jamila tells her friends Alejandra and Campbell. They shut their faucets off, too!

The Brownie friends tell their class what they are doing. All the kids work together on a project to really **SAVE** water!

The class **SHARES** what they are learning and doing about water with the whole school. So the whole school gets inspired, too.

The kids at the school **SHARE** what they are learning and doing with kids at all the other schools in their state. Now all the kids across the state are inspired to . . .

And then . . .

When people **LOVE WATER**, work together to **SAVE** it, and then **SHARE** what they know with even more people, here's what happens:

Your very own Brownie Team story! Show and tell your story of how you **LOVE** water, how your team worked together to **SAVE** water, and how you went on to **SHARE** what you learned to get others protecting water, too!
Use your imagination! Maybe you can make one giant story with your team.

I **LOVE** water because . . .

I learned to show my **LOVE** by . . .

Then our whole Brownie Team decided to . . .

That's important because . . .

We **SAVED** water by . . .

But we weren't done . . .

We **SHARED** what we were doing with _____

And now . . .

SAVE and SHARE: What Brownies Can Do

The Brownies can choose from a variety of projects for their SAVE and SHARE awards. Here are project ideas featured in the girls' book and how girls can turn them into efforts that SAVE and SHARE as they become advocates for the wise use of water. With your guidance, the girls will come up with even more project ideas.

Project	How Brownies Can Save Water	How Brownies Can Share Water
Shut Off That Faucet!	Get permission to post signs (at home, school, library, Girl Scout properties, place of worship) that encourage people to turn off the faucet—as in washing properly without using more water than they need. Aim for clever slogans, like "Don't Drip a Single Drop!"	They find out how much water is SAVED by their efforts. They SHARE what they've done with those in charge of the buildings they've helped. They inspire others to join in the effort.
Ban Plastic Water Bottles!	Get others to stop buying them. Ask them to drink from reusable containers instead. Ask classmates, schools, sports teams, neighbors, even the whole community.	They let even more people know what they've accomplished. They might influence store owners in their area to stop selling small bottles of water, too.
Grow Water-Smart Plants	Ask those in charge of the plantings (at neighborhood parks, school, the community) to replace water-hungry plants with ones that live naturally in your area with little water.	They SHARE their effort to make others aware of the water they might be wasting. It will get them thinking about how to SAVE water and inspire them to join in the effort.
Choose a Broom, Not a Hose	Encourage neighbors, schools, and businesses to stop hosing down sidewalks and driveways and to start sweeping instead.	Tell those in charge of your town how many people have agreed to put down their hoses. Spread the word and get even more people to join in!

Thinking Ahead to the Final WOW! Award

The last award the Brownies will earn, the WOW! award, is tied to all the Brownies will be doing from here on out. As the girls SAVE and SHARE, they will see how they can create change. That's an important part of what they will be learning. So think of ways for them to understand the impact of what they are doing. Creating sign-up sheets for participants, taking photos of their efforts, and connecting with the media may all be part of the girls' process for earning WOW! They can also obtain proof of their impact from:

- letters from community members who saw positive change happen

- before-and-after photos of a solved problem and the people affected

- a list of signatures of people who promised to join in their effort

- a report in the school or PTA bulletin about their accomplishments

- a news article about their project

- a certificate from those they inspired

- a scrapbook documenting their influence

The girls' personal statement of how their effort relates to the Girl Scout Law can be documented, too, and shared visually as well as orally as part of the award ceremony and the close of the *WOW!* journey.

SAMPLE SESSION 5
Advocates Communicate!

AT A GLANCE

Goal: The Brownie Team continues to prepare for its SAVE effort, making any visual aids they need and practicing some key speaking points they need as advocates. They engage in a fun communication game (a special version of charades) and create their own "Communication Tips for Advocating."

- Opening Ceremony: Brownies Around the World
- Communicate It!
- Preparing to SAVE
- Closing Ceremony: Water and Animals

MATERIALS

- Arts and crafts supplies for the SAVE effort (posters, signs, etc.)
- "Communicate It!" slips for girls to choose from a bag and act out (copy from page 81 of this session)
- Poster board, cardboard, or large sheet of paper and marker to capture the "Communication Tips for Advocating"

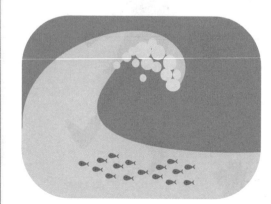

- Photocopy the "Communicate It!" scenarios from page 81 and cut them into individual slips or tape them to index cards. Or better yet, copy the scenarios onto strips of used or recycled paper. Fold the strips so they can't be read, or place them in a bowl or bag for girls to choose from.

- Arrange for a helper or two to be on hand from the Brownie Friends and Family Network to assist the girls as they interpret and act out their "Communicate It!" scenario.

AS GIRLS ARRIVE

Take out the WOW map with the team plan that the girls added at the last gathering. Is there anything else the girls want to add?

Opening Ceremony: Brownies Around the World

Ask the girls if they know how many Girl Scout Brownies there are across the country (about 800,000!) and around the world (many, many more!). Let them know that Girl Scouts is part of the World Association of Girl Guides and Girl Scouts, with members in countries all over the globe.

Now ask: *Do you know what that means? You—Brownies—are a powerful force in the world! Imagine what you can accomplish! Can you imagine Brownies gathered in a circle in the next state? In another country? Maybe even all around the world?*

Then say something like: *A big part of using your Brownie power for the good of Earth is being confident about speaking up. What do you think confidence means?*

Gather some ideas from the girls and then help summarize, saying: *Confidence means believing in who you are and believing that what you say and do can affect others—for the better! That's advocating!*

IF YOUR GROUP IS LARGE . . .

Divide into groups of 5-10 girls and give each group its own bowl of slips, allowing everyone to fully participate.

USE HUMOR!

Encourage the girls to really "do it up" and exaggerate the role they are playing. Humor is a great tool for learning! Once girls get the idea of the role, they don't need to use the exact words that are on their slip.

Communicate It!

Let the girls know that as they work to SAVE water, they'll have many opportunities to share what they know with others. As they speak with other people, they'll be advocating for water by asking them to SAVE water, too.

Ask the girls to recap their chosen SAVE project and make a list of who they will need to talk to. Keep this list in mind throughout the activity so you can work in specific examples that help link the game to the girls' "real" project.

Ask the girls to check out the "Tips for Talking" WOW on pages 54–55 of their book. Ask: What do you think of these tips? Are you ready to come up with some more tips of your own?

Now, explain the "Communicate It!" game to the Brownies:

- *It's a little like charades, where each girl chooses a slip from the bag and acts out the character written on the slip.*

- *Have fun! Exaggerate if you want to! Play the role to the max!*

- *The other girls have to think about the communication problems this character has.*

- *Then the team thinks of a good Communication Tip for Advocating and adds it to their master list.*

Be sure to emphasize that this is a game! Let the girls know that in real life, it's not polite to give people nicknames like these!

PLAY IT OUT

Ask for a girl to volunteer to be the first to choose a slip from the bowl. Have a helper take the volunteer aside and assist her in interpreting the role she will act out for the group. Meanwhile, say to the rest of the Brownies: *Pretend you are a group of people whom we are trying to inspire and encourage to join us in saving water. Listen and observe how _____ talks to you. Does her way of talking make you want to join the effort? Think about what would make the communication better.*

After each girl plays her role for the group, guide a mini-discussion by asking the Brownie Team questions like:

- *How did you feel when _____ talked to you?*
- *Did _____ make you feel like you want and need to SAVE water?*

- *What would you call that way of communicating? (Let the team guess and then invite the "actress" to name her character.)*

- *Why do we sometimes act this way?*

- *What are some ideas you have for communicating better? How will these help you to be a successful advocate?*

After each mini-discussion, invite the Brownies to come up with one "Top Tip for Advocating" that they will follow as a team. Ask a helper to capture each tip in a short phrase on a large piece of paper or poster. Keep these Brownie Tips for Advocating handy as a reminder for everything else Brownies do as they go on to SAVE and SHARE.

ROUND 2!

Time permitting, the girls might like to try a "Do Over" round in which they take turns acting out the best use of their Top Tips for Advocating.

Preparing to SAVE

Now the girls will likely need time to create materials or presentations for their SAVE effort. They might be designing signs to hang in a school about not running water longer than needed, practicing how to ask people to use refillable water bottles, or making a presentation to ask everyone in their neighborhood to check for leaks.

- Organize the girls to work on whatever might be needed for the team's SAVE efforts—signs, booklets, a skit, etc.

- Or invite the girls to talk with a special visitor whose work or volunteer effort is related to the Brownies' SAVE project. For example, perhaps someone from the local water utility.

As the Brownies plan their effort, guide them to promote good teamwork by:

- Encouraging them to take turns

- Making sure each girl has a role

- Praising girls when you observe great cooperation

POOF!

Closing Ceremony: Water and Animals

After all the good work the Brownies have done today, they might enjoy this fun and active ceremony in which each girl thinks of an animal that uses water in a special way and then acts out that animal's behavior as the other girls try to guess what animal she is.

Gather the girls in a Brownie Circle. Say:

- *We've played a version of charades about people—now let's play charades about animals.*

- *We've been discovering how all animals need water to survive and they often use it in different ways.*

- *In the ELF Adventure in the wetlands, the beaver uses water to send a warning. It slaps its tail against the water to tell other beavers of possible danger.*

- *Think for a few minutes about an animal you know and how it uses water. Perhaps this animal drinks in a special way. Or perhaps it uses water to help it find food. Don't tell anyone what animal you picked.*

- *Each of you will act out how your animal uses water and the rest of us will try to guess your animal.*

Then invite the girls to go around the circle, taking turns imitating their chosen animal.

Communicate It! Scenarios

Miss Mumbly: Umm . . . you know, it's kind of like, ummm, well, maybe . . . you umm don't need to have that ahhhh umm plastic umm bottle ahh all the time (Hint: Speak in a low voice, look down, seem lost. Stop a lot between the words.)

Miss Unkind: Hey! Don't you see all that water running down the sink? What's wrong with you! You are so bad and wrong! (Hint: Be very loud and kind of scary.)

Miss 2Q (Too Quiet): You know people in Africa don't have enough water to drink. It would be really nice if we all saved more water. (Hint: Whisper and look down.)

Miss I Dunno: Water is important. I don't really remember why. I don't really get it. But it is, so just don't waste it, OK? (Hint: Act like you haven't learned anything!)

Miss Silent (Say Nothing): (What happens if you say nothing on behalf of Earth's water?)

Miss Gum Chewer: Chew away—loudly! While you say, "Water. We need to save it. Can you shut the faucet off, please!" (Hint: Pretend to be chewing gum—in a big way!)

Miss Messy: I have something really important to tell you about Earth's water. If we don't stop wasting it we're going to be in big trouble! (Hint: Mess up clothes and hair . . . look like you just crawled out of bed.)

Miss Who Cares: Well, yesterday, I went shopping and got this great new shirt. And also, look, I have my own TV. I am having pizza for dinner. And oh, by the way, you really should do something about the water problem.

Miss Unbelievable: I like to carry my own plastic water bottle that is new from the store every day. I really need it. I also need to take really long showers and run the faucet when I brush my teeth. I just have to. But you—you really better not do stuff like this! (Hint: Act like you don't have to help, but everyone else does!)

SAVE!

This session plan assumes the Brownies are working on their SAVE project. Depending on the nature of the project and the time available to the team, they might be planning the project, creating materials for it (booklets, posters, or displays), talking to water experts, or taking a field trip.

AT A GLANCE

Goal: The girls team up to carry out the challenge they have set for themselves with the SAVE project.

- Opening Ceremony: Making a Difference

- SAVE Project

- Option: The Watery World of Watercolor

- Closing Ceremony

- Looking Ahead to Session 7

MATERIALS

- Whatever the Brownie Team needs to carry out its SAVE project and/or supplies for any of the creative options they choose to do.

- **The Watery World of Watercolor:** Watercolor paints, cups of water, watercolor paper or any paper for painting, newspapers to cover tables or other painting surfaces.

PREPARE AHEAD

- Reach out to the Brownie Friends and Family Network to ensure that there are enough rides and helpers available for project day.

- Talk to those in charge of wherever the SAVE effort is taking place to review any logistics:

- Do key staff know the girls are putting up signs by the faucets or making a presentation about stopping leaks?

- Are families aware that they will be asked to stop using bottled water?

- Do those in charge of the library or place of worship know the Brownie Team will be requesting new practices for cleaning driveways or planting gardens that use less water?

You get the idea! Based on your team's plan, pave the way for the Brownies' effort!

Options: For some extra fun, add in the art activity at the end of this session. Girls might also like to spend some group time on activities in their *WOW!* book, including: "What Will You Design?" on page 53 (which gets the girls thinking like an engineer) or "Imagine Your Own Sub for Underwater Adventures" on page 63.

AS GIRLS ARRIVE

Invite girls to set up the watercolor materials or to add more details to their Team WOW Map.

PROVIDE ENCOURAGEMENT AND PERSPECTIVE

Sometimes the "nitty-gritties" of the girls' effort to SAVE water may feel small or unimportant. So as the Brownies wait to see if others will truly follow up on their requests, be sure to lift the team's spirits! You might:

- Remind the girls that making the world better is often about getting a small snowball moving or just planting a seed. You might not see results right away, but you know you are getting something good started!

- Encourage the girls to keep at it. If responses to their efforts are not yet strong, they might adjust their initial idea in some way and try again! (See "Time for a WOW: Patience and Persistence" on page 106 of the girls' book.)

- Highlight positive aspects of the girls' effort: Well, the school can't _____ right now, but you gave great ideas for the future!

Opening Ceremony: Making a Difference

Before the SAVE effort begins, gather the Brownies together and ask: *What is the Girl Scout Motto?*

Be Prepared!

Right! And as a team we have prepared for this effort to SAVE water.

Then ask each girl to make one statement about the purpose of the team's project. It may help to provide a sample statement for the girls to speak to, such as:

Our SAVE project is important because _____.

SAVE Project

Get to it! Engage the girls in carrying out their plan. Remind them that no matter what their project—whether they are asking adults "in charge" to start a new habit for a school, library, or place of worship, or posting "don't run it too long" signs by faucets, or urging people to stop buying plastic bottles of water, or doing something else altogether—they are actively working together to SAVE water!

Optional: The Watery World of Watercolor

Water plays a role in many arts and crafts, from painting to papier-mâché. If the team has time during their SAVE efforts, invite the girls to go all out and have some fun with watery paints.

- Cover the tables with several thicknesses of newspaper.

- Distribute a small, reusable cup of water to each girl.

- Encourage the girls to experiment with adding more and less water to their paints so they can observe how the amount of water changes the intensity of each paint's color.

- Encourage them to find a whole spectrum of color, such as pale pink to bright red! Also encourage them to mix colors to create new ones.

- You might suggest that the Brownies paint their favorite water place, or an ocean or river or lake scene with flowers and plant life.

- Or they might simply play with dripping colors from above the paper.

- If they want something "official" to create, they could make their Save Water certificates now (see "If Time Permits," page 87) instead of waiting until the next session.

Closing Ceremony

Before the Brownies head home, invite them into a circle and share this quote from Brownie Elf (from page 14 of the girls' book):

"Water's journey never really ends. It's a circle that keeps going around, like bicycle wheels. No beginning and no end. That's why it's called the water cycle."

Then compare the water cycle to the journey you and the girls are on. You might say: *Just like water, our journey never really ends! We will keep on thinking and acting to save and protect water. And each time, we will make progress and learn something new!*

Invite the girls to join hands in a Friendship Circle. Then encourage them to go around the circle one by one, each saying a positive risk she took while saving water and what she learned from the experience.

Looking Ahead to Session 7

Encourage the girls to check out these "Time for a WOW!" activities in their book: "Inspiring Others" (page 85) or "Share What You Know and Get Others to Join in, Too! (pages 100–101).

Ask them to think about all they have learned and done, and what they will ask others to do for water! Perhaps they would like to add some new images or thoughts to their Team WOW Map to capture the SAVE effort they've now completed.

**MISTAKE?
NO PROBLEM!**

Mistakes are a great way for girls to learn. And often they result in something truly creative! Invite the Brownies to talk about what went wrong and why, and what they can do differently next time now that they've learned something new!

SAMPLE SESSION 7
Planning to SHARE

AT A GLANCE

Goal: The Brownies earn the SAVE Water Award as they reflect on all they accomplished through their project. They go on to plan to SHARE what they have learned, to educate and inspire other people, so that even more people will protect the right of Earth and all people to clean water!

- Opening Ceremony: Earning the SAVE Water Award
- Pass It On
- Get Creative
- Closing Ceremony: Drop to River, River to Ocean

MATERIALS

- Team WOW Map
- SAVE Water awards
- Paper and art supplies, or watercolor work from previous session

PREPARE AHEAD

Read over "Saving and Protecting Water" on pages 56–59 of the girls' book. Focus on the SAVE and SHARE examples. Now that the girls have acted as a team to SAVE Water, who else can they SHARE their effort with to get even more people acting on behalf of water?

AS GIRLS ARRIVE

Encourage girls to look again at these Time for a WOW! activities in their book: "Inspiring Others" on page 85 or "Share What You Know and Get Others to Join in, Too!" on page 100–101. Ask them to think about what they've learned and done that they will ask others to do, too.

The Brownies might also like to add some new ideas or images to their Team WOW Map to capture the SAVE effort they've now completed.

Opening Ceremony: Earning the SAVE Award

Let the girls know what you believe they accomplished on behalf of Earth's water. Give them examples of the good teamwork you saw in action, too!

Ask:

- *Would you like to give yourselves a round of applause?*
- *Or pat one another on the back?*

They might like to recite one of the water-loving Brownie chants they learned earlier in their journey:

> *Careful, careful with each drop!*
> *There is no more, so waste must stop!*

Or maybe they have their own special way to savor the moment!

Now present each girl with her SAVE Water Award and invite her to say in her own words what she has achieved. You might choose or adapt one of the following statements and post it on a big sheet of paper to aid girls as they consider what to say:

- The most important thing I learned during our SAVE project is . . .
- I am proud of our SAVE project because we advocated by speaking up about . . .
- I think our SAVE project is important because . . .

IF TIME PERMITS . . .

Invite each girl to use paper and art supplies, or her watercolor work from the previous session, to make a SAVE Water certificate for herself. On it, she can write her response to one or all of the accomplishment statements. Alternatively, girls might like to draw a certificate in their books, on their Wonders of Water map (pages 30–31).

PRIDE = SELF-CONFIDENCE

Be sure to let the team know how proud you are of their efforts to SAVE Earth's water. Letting the girls know the value of their project and the quality of their work builds their confidence and encourages them to keep on going—now and on future efforts, whether for water or anything else!

WHERE TO SHARE?

Girls might even conduct their SHARE effort during the school day (or at lunchtime or early in the morning). They would just need to ask permission to round up some other students and their teachers or parents to participate.

Pass It On

Ask the girls to turn to page 95 of their book and read them the story excerpt (or invite the Brownies to take turns reading it!) that begins with Brownie Elf saying, "We have to find ways to protect the animals and help people" and ends (on page 98) with "We'll always remember what you taught us. We'll pass it on all our lives."

Then say: *We have a chance in real life to do what the Brownie friends in our story are doing! Now that we have saved water and gotten some other people involved, we can think even bigger! Who else can we tell about our efforts to save water?* Ask the girls to write down ideas; give them prompts as needed. Those they will now SHARE their efforts with might include family members (parents, aunts, uncles, cousins, grandparents), neighbors, teachers, classmates, the school principal and staff, local businesses or restaurants, other Girl Scouts (volunteers and girls), younger kids at school or in Girl Scouts.

Once girls have made a list, guide them to think about who they will have the most success inviting into their water effort. Together, you and the girls can contact some of these people to come to the SHARE effort. (After the session, see who in the Brownie Friends and Family Network can help you reach out.) You don't need an army of people (though that's always nice!). You just need a group of people the girls can educate and inspire to take action for water.

Get Creative

Now turn the girls' attention to *how* they will educate and inspire this group. Get the girls preparing and practicing what they will say to their guests. They might say something like this:

When our Brownie team follows the Girl Scout Law, we have an impact! On this WOW journey, we have each taken action to love water as individuals and we've come together as a team to do a project that saves water.

But just like when we say the Girl Scout Law together it feels even more powerful, our efforts to save water will be even more powerful when we all work on them together.

So today, we are going to SHARE what we have been doing for water with you and ask you to do it, too!

Once the girls have their message ready, they might also enjoy:

- making up a fun slogan or motto that captures their effort

- creating a short commercial or advertisement or a short play or puppet show to act out ways to save water

- grabbing the attention of others with a song ("We all live in a . . . ")

- each holding up a poster board with a simple message about why water needs us

- testing their guests with some of the quiz questions they've encountered in their books

- showing a visual representation of how much of the Earth's water is drinkable/or that one in six people on Earth do not have enough water (see the pictures on pages 24 and 52 of their book)

- inviting their guests to visit stations where they have to try to carry or use water the way families do in places where water is scarce (like the activities the team did in Sessions 2 and 3 of their journey)

As the girls' SHARE project takes shape, talk to them about what kind of opening ceremony they might use at their event. They might like to play up the water drop idea from Session 8, page 92.

Closing: Drop to River, River to Ocean

Remind the girls of how the journey began with their personal efforts to love water. Then, they teamed up for their SAVE project. You might say, this is kind of like the way little bits of water pick up speed and power and form a river! And where do rivers flow? Into the ocean! We have now gone from saving a little water, to saving more water—and now we are going to share what we have been learning and doing with even more people. In this way, our efforts to save Earth's water can become as powerful as an ocean!

Now, invite the girls to start a little chant: *Water Drop to River, River to Ocean!* Suggest that they start softly, and then chant louder and louder—just like the roar of an ocean!

HOW BIG A PROJECT?

NOT MUCH TIME?

Guide the team toward an imaginative way of "sharing" that does not require a lot of advance preparation. What matters is that the girls have a chance to share what they've learned and then invite others to take action for water, too.

For example, the girls could set up stations using materials they have already prepared throughout their journey. A station could be as simple as an open page of their *WOW!* book, the Team WOW Map, or photos of the team in action. Pairs of girls could host each station.

PLENTY OF TIME?

If the Brownie Team can add a few sessions to the journey (and has enough helpers!), the team might go all out with a play or puppet show that acts out how a character wastes water and then learns how important it is to LOVE water and takes action to SAVE it. The team could make invitations to their event, plan refreshments to serve, and "ELF it up" in any way they like.

SHARE!

AT A GLANCE

Goal: The Brownie Team carries out its plan to educate others about what they have done to LOVE and SAVE water, and inspires others to join in their effort by loving and saving water, too. The session concludes with the girls earning their SHARE Water award.

- Opening Ceremony: River to Ocean
- Educate and Inspire
- Making a Promise

- Closing Ceremony: Earning SHARE Water
- Looking Ahead to Session 9

MATERIALS

- Visual materials girls have decided to use
- Water drops for the guests' water promise

- Girl Scout Law written in large print on a chalkboard or poster (or copied for guests onto recycled materials)
- SHARE Water awards

PREPARE AHEAD

- Reach out to the Brownie Friends and Family Network and any other people the Brownies have identified for their SHARE effort. Enthusiastically remind everyone that the Brownie Team needs their participation or they won't have anyone to educate and inspire!

- Set up some of the materials that highlight what the Brownie Team has been up to along the journey so guests can view them as they arrive. The Team WOW Map, water drops, and photos of the Brownie Team in action are all good possibilities.

AS GIRLS ARRIVE

Remind them that today they have guests arriving. Ask for volunteers to greet the guests and help organize the various steps of the gathering, including explaining the SHARE Water project.

Opening Ceremony: River to Ocean

Invite the girls to form an inner circle as the guests they will educate and inspire form an outer circle around them. (Perhaps a Brownie can give these instructions and teach the guests the Girl Scout Quiet Sign, too!)

Ask the girls to say the Girl Scout Law. Now ask them to repeat it, but this time, the outer circle needs to say it with them, loudly and with energy! (They can read it on the inside cover of their book or from the newsprint you may have posted.)

The Brownies who have volunteered to explain the SHARE project to the guests can now deliver the message they've been practicing to say to their guests, ending with something like:

So today, we are going to SHARE what we have been doing for water with you and ask you to do it, too!

Educate and Inspire

Now it's time for the Brownies to "show and tell" their guests what they have learned about the importance of protecting water, and the ways in which they have begun to LOVE and SAVE it.

Guide the Brownies as they put their "Plan to SHARE" into motion as a team. Perhaps they are performing a play or puppet show, using posterboards to describe how they have acted for water, describing their efforts with photos, or pursuing whatever creative ideas you have guided them to bring to life.

Making a Promise

Now that the girls have educated and inspired their guests, they are ready to ask them to make a commitment to take action and save water, too.

Encourage the Brownies to pass the water drops out to their guests and ask them to write down their promise for saving water. The Brownies can use their know-how to offer some hints and ideas!

Once all guests have made a promise, they can join the team in posting their water drops in "the ocean"— a giant posterboard, bulletin board, box, or whatever format you have chosen together, to tape or otherwise attach all the droplets.

The girls can encourage each guest to say what she will do to help SHARE in this effort to SAVE water as she posts her drop.

Closing Ceremony: Earning SHARE Water

Invite the Brownie Team members to stand in front of the ocean of action for water that they have created. Then encourage each girl to complete this statement as you present the SHARE Water award to her:

With more of us promising to save water, Earth and all people and animals will _____.

(Consider posting the statement where everyone can see it. Another option is for the Brownies—and all their guests—to choose one response that they all say together: loudly!)

TREATS AND WONDERS

Depending on the time available and the girls' plans, perhaps they want to share some water treats or spend some time sharing more Wonders of Water with their guests. Rainbow-making? Water-song festival? "Green" Tea for a Blue Planet?

Looking Ahead to Session 9

How would the girls like to celebrate the journey? Ask them to check out the "Time to Celebrate' section on page 110 of their book. Do they want to have a tea party for their water friends? Sing watery songs? Enjoy the WOW of making rainbows? Is the weather good for an outdoor celebration? Will they invite special guests and share their Team WOW Map? Remind the girls to bring their special jars with water from their favorite water places. They'll use them in a special closing ceremony for this *WOW!* journey!

The notes for this session offer ideas about how to celebrate *WOW!* while encouraging girls to feel great about all they have learned and done as protectors of Earth's water—and as members of a Brownie Team. Adjust these ideas according to the interests of your Brownie Team. Coordinate support with the Brownie Friends and Family Network.

MORE BROWNIES, MORE WOW!

Earth's systems work best when biodiversity is in play, and so, too, do human systems. When we include others of diverse backgrounds and experiences in order to learn from and give to one another, everyone benefits.

So consider linking the final WOW! celebration to the ceremonies of other Brownie teams in your region. That way, the girls can celebrate even more WOWs! The girls might enjoy a cooperative game to get to know one another, and even their seating arrangements for the festivities can include meeting a new Brownie friend.

Ask your Girl Scout council for assistance in linking up with Brownie teams whose hometowns, race, ethnicity, and/or faith will bring diversity to the celebration.

WOW!

AT A GLANCE

Goal: Girls take pride in the ways they have challenged themselves to learn and grow as advocates who speak and act on behalf of water and people—and in their ways of working as a team.

- Opening Ceremony: It's the Law!
- Gifts of Leadership
- Sharing Our Special Water Places
- WOW! Awards
- Celebrate!
- Imagining What Happens Next

MATERIALS

- Watery Treat Refreshments (note the melon "cookies" on page 111 of the girls' book)
- WOW! awards
- Water friends or pets (or supplies for any activities the team has chosen)
- Visuals from the journey (Team WOW Map, water drops, SAVE photos, etc.)

PREPARE AHEAD

Think back on all the Brownies have accomplished—both related to Wonders of Water and Ways of Working. Be ready to remind them of how they succeeded. If possible, plan to display some visual "proof" of the girls' efforts, making use of the suggested methods on page 75 of this guide.

AS GIRLS ARRIVE

Encourage them to greet their guests and take turns sharing the details of their Team WOW Map and any other journey items they've chosen to display.

Opening Ceremony: It's the Law!

Invite the girls to make a circle around their Team WOW Map and say the Girl Scout Promise and Law together. Then ask the team to give examples of how they have acted on some of the values of the Law during this journey. It might help them to look at the words of the Law on the inside front cover of their book.

"Using resources wisely" may be mentioned right away! Encourage girls to reflect on other ways they have lived the Law, too. Offer the girls a few prompts to remind them of all their accomplishments.

- Perhaps they have been a sister to other Girl Scouts (through some of their Ways of Working).

- They may have been courageous and strong (by speaking up the right way or trying something new).

- Or maybe they were responsible for what they say and do (by following up on their plans).

Gifts of Leadership

Invite the girls to pair up and give each pair a spot to sit in. Ask each girl to think of a way her partner has acted like a leader on this journey. What talents and qualities has she brought to the team? Encourage the partners to share their ideas about each other's leadership. You might offer a few examples, such as:

Perhaps your partner took responsibility for setting up something? Or she made something we all enjoyed? Shared her special talent for

_____? *Helped us with* _____?

Give each girl a water drop (or a piece of paper) and ask the girls to write down one way in which their partners are leaders.

Gather the team together again and have each girl say why she thinks her partner has been a leader as she presents the water drop/slip of paper to her as a gift. Girls might like to add this drop to their *WOW!* books as a keepsake.

Sharing Our Special Water Places

Now ask the girls to gather their water jars and return to their circle. Invite them to go around the circle, reminding one another (and letting their guests hear!) of their favorite water place. Ask them to say one new thing they've learned about their special water place while being on this *WOW!* journey.

WOW! Awards

Now, present each girl with her WOW! Award and let the guests see the signs of their impact, using the "proof" the girls have gathered (using tips on page 75). Then . . .

...Celebrate!

Bring out the water friends and watery treats. Invite the girls to introduce their animal friends to one another. What can they share about their habits?

Or perhaps girls are using this last gathering to make their own water pet! Check out the celebration ideas on pages 110–111 of their book.

Add in some favorite songs about water, too! Check out the lyrics to "My Paddle," on page 35 of the girls' book, or try that old favorite, "Barges."

And how about photos and autographs? A team photo around the WOW Map would make a nice memento for the journey. So would autographs. Perhaps the girls would like to sign one another's books and add a memory, too!

Imagining What Happens Next

If the Brownie Team will continue on with other Girl Scout adventures this year, spend a few minutes at the conclusion of the celebration getting the girls excited about what's to come. If this concludes the experience of these Brownies for the year, engage the girls in thinking about how they will participate in Girl Scouts next year. A new journey? Camping? Other events going on through your Girl Scout council? Be sure the girls (and their Friends and Family Network!) know how to keep their Girl Scout adventures growing!

To really get the girls thinking about what's possible as they grow up in Girl Scouts, invite them to check out the "Ocean Lover" story on page 68 of their book. It's about 16-year-old Girl Scout Katherine Fondacaro. Ask the girls to imagine the Girl Scout adventures they might enjoy when they are 16!

Then take some time give *yourself* a really big WOW! That was some journey! Also look back at your thoughts about leadership on page 28. What new thoughts do you now have? What leadership WOWS will you now share?